Parenting After Emotional Neglect

A Cycle-Breaking Guide to Raising Emotionally Seen Children While Healing Yourself

Clara Rowan Fielding

This book provides general educational information about parenting, emotional responsiveness, family patterns, and personal reflection. It is not medical, mental health, legal, or other professional advice, and it does not replace assessment or treatment from a qualified professional who can consider an individual child, adult, or family.

No particular result is promised. Readers remain responsible for decisions made in their own circumstances. Seek appropriate local help for persistent impairment, suspected abuse, domestic violence, custody questions, or concerns about a child's development or health. Contact local emergency or crisis services when anyone may be in immediate danger.

Names, family details, and scenarios in this book are composites created for teaching. They are not intended to portray, diagnose, or misrepresent any identifiable person or family.

ISBN: 978-1-911838-27-2

Contents

Preface

Parenting can bring an old childhood rule back to life in seconds. A child cries, clings, refuses, or needs comfort, and the adult who once survived by having few needs can feel trapped, sharp, blank, or ashamed. Most parenting books begin with what the child needs. Most recovery books begin with what happened to the adult. These pages stay with the collision between the two.

Emotional neglect refers here to a repeated lack of adequate emotional noticing, response, guidance, or comfort during childhood. It is not defined by a single missed cue, a tired parent, or an ordinary family conflict. It can occur in homes that look organized and responsible from the outside. A child may be fed, educated, and protected while learning that sadness is inconvenient, anger is unacceptable, dependence is embarrassing, or help should not be requested. Those lessons can remain quiet until parenting brings them into daily contact with another person's needs.

The central difficulty is not simply that a parent lacks the right script. A child's crying, refusal, clinginess, disappointment, or demand for attention can activate an old rule before the thinking mind has time to catch up. The adult can become sharp, go blank, overexplain, give in, or leave emotionally while remaining physically present. Advice such as "stay calm" does little when the body reads the moment as danger, engulfment, failure, or shame.

This book offers a structured way to work with that collision. Its central framework, the Two-Story Pause, asks you to separate the child's present story from the old story that has awakened in you. From there, you learn to see the emotion, hold the necessary limit, choose a response your nervous system can actually carry out, and return after mistakes. The goal is not a home without frustration. It is a home in which feelings can be acknowledged, limits can remain firm, and disconnection is followed by honest repair.

The book is written primarily for current and prospective parents who recognize emotional neglect in their own history. It may also be useful to stepparents, foster and adoptive parents, grandparents, and co-parents who want to understand why ordinary dependency can feel unusually difficult. Examples are composites. They are designed to show patterns rather than portray identifiable people.

This is educational guidance, not diagnosis or treatment. It cannot assess a child, determine whether a family is safe, or replace support from a pediatrician, licensed mental health professional, school specialist, or other qualified provider. It also does not promise that insight will erase old reactions. Change usually comes through repeated, imperfect practice, along with support when the burden is too great to carry privately.

The purpose of these pages is simple: help you remain the adult your child needs without abandoning the adult you are still learning to care for.

Introduction

Maya was kneeling beside the bathtub when her four-year-old began crying because the blue cup was in the dishwasher. The red cup was clean. The water was warm. Nothing was wrong in any practical sense. Maya heard herself say, "This is ridiculous," with the same flat impatience she remembered from childhood.

Her daughter cried harder. Maya felt heat rise in her chest. A second voice appeared inside her: You are doing it again. You are becoming your mother.

That second voice did not make her gentler. It made her frightened, and fear made her faster. She offered three cups, promised a story, threatened to end bath time, and finally walked into the hall. The whole episode lasted less than five minutes. It stayed with her for days.

Many parents who grew up with emotional neglect know this kind of moment. The child's need is ordinary, but the parent's reaction feels out of proportion. Then shame arrives and turns one difficult exchange into evidence of a permanent flaw. The parent may spend the evening researching better responses, only to discover that knowledge disappears when the next cry lands on the same old wound.

This book starts from a different premise. Your reaction is not the whole truth about your parenting. It is information. It may tell you that a particular sound, demand, facial expression, or kind of dependency is linked to an old rule. It may tell you that you are overloaded, unsupported, hungry, rushed, or scared. It may tell you that the child needs less explanation and more containment. Information can be used. Shame usually cannot.

The Two Stories in the Room

Every charged parenting moment contains at least two stories.

The first is the child's present story. A preschooler may be tired and unable to shift plans. A seven-year-old may be ashamed after making a mistake. A teenager may be protecting dignity by sounding dismissive. The child's behavior is not the entire story, but it is the visible part.

The second is the parent's old story. This is the rule your system learned about emotion and need. Do not make a fuss. Handle it yourself. Anger is dangerous. Crying is manipulation. A good child is easy. A good parent fixes everything. These rules often arrive as certainty rather than memory.

The Two-Story Pause is the practice of telling those stories apart before choosing your next move. It uses four questions:

> *What is happening in the room right now?*

What old rule or fear has awakened in me?

What does my child need from the adult in this moment?

What is the smallest steady action I can take next?

You may answer those questions in 20 seconds, later that evening, or the following day. The pause is not a performance of perfect calm. It is a break in automaticity. Sometimes it leads to a warm response. Sometimes it leads to a simple limit spoken without contempt. Sometimes it leads to repair after the moment has already gone badly.

Research does not support a simple claim that a parent's childhood automatically determines how that parent will behave. A systematic review found intergenerational associations across several parenting domains, but it also found considerable variation, which matters because risk is not destiny (Greene et al., 2020). Reviews of emotion-focused parenting programs likewise suggest that parents can learn more supportive ways of responding to children's emotions, while the size and consistency of effects vary across studies and outcomes (England-Mason et al., 2023; Havighurst et al., 2020).

That is the stance of this book: your history matters, and it is not a verdict.

What Emotionally Seen Means

An emotionally seen child is not a constantly happy child. The phrase does not mean that a parent agrees with every feeling, prevents every disappointment, or turns the household around each emotional wave. It means the child repeatedly receives evidence that inner experience can be noticed without ridicule, fear, or withdrawal.

Being seen can sound like, "You wanted one more turn, and stopping is hard."

It can also sound like, "I believe that you are furious. I will not let you hit."

The first sentence acknowledges experience. The second adds protection. Both are forms of emotional responsiveness.

Responsive caregiving involves back-and-forth attention to a child's signals, especially in early development. The Center on the Developing Child at Harvard describes these exchanges as "serve and return" and emphasizes that responsive interaction supports developing communication and social capacities. The useful lesson for a parent is not that every signal must receive an ideal response. It is that relationships are built through repeated exchanges in which the child reaches and the adult, often enough, returns (Center on the Developing Child at Harvard University, n.d.).

What This Book Will Not Ask

You will not be asked to excuse the adults who failed you. Understanding a pattern is not the same as forgiving it, reconciling with someone, or deciding that harm did not matter.

You will not be asked to tell your child details they are not developmentally ready to hold. Repair is about taking responsibility for your behavior, not asking the child to comfort you about your childhood.

You will not be asked to become endlessly available. Children need boundaries, predictable structure, privacy, sleep, work, adult relationships, and parents who can say no. Emotional responsiveness is not the removal of limits. It is the refusal to use disconnection as the limit.

You will not be asked to judge your family by a single scene. Patterns matter more than snapshots. A tired response can be repaired. A rushed morning does not define a home. The same is true of improvement: one excellent conversation does not replace daily practice.

How to Use These Pages

The chapters move in three stages. The first helps you understand activation and build a workable pause. The second applies the approach to validation, limits, tears, anger, and growing independence. The third focuses on repair, overcorrection, co-parenting, development, family culture, and professional support.

Each chapter includes scripts and a practice tool. Use them as starting points, not lines you must recite perfectly. A sentence that sounds natural in one family can feel artificial in another. The principle matters more than the exact words.

Read slowly enough to notice where you become defensive, relieved, sad, or skeptical. Those reactions may point to the old rules most in need of attention. Choose one practice at a time. A household does not become responsive because a parent remembers 40 techniques. It changes when one different response becomes available under stress, then another.

The standard throughout is not perfection. It is enough steadiness to see what is happening, enough honesty to own what happened, and enough repetition for a child to learn that connection can survive difficulty.

A Quick Route Through the Book

You do not need to read every chapter before using a tool. If a difficult moment has just happened, Chapter 10 helps with repair. For tears or separation, go to Chapter 7; for anger or aggression, Chapter 8; for limits that keep collapsing, Chapters 6 and 11; for conflict with another adult, Chapter 12; and for concerns that are persistent, severe, worsening, or affecting daily life, Chapter 15.

Read the Introduction and Chapters 1 through 3 first when you want the full framework. Then choose the chapter that matches the pattern showing up most often. Return to the appendices when you need a script, a written map, or a short plan you can use during an ordinary week.

Chapter 1: When Need Feels Dangerous

Daniel was carrying groceries through the front door when his two-year-old wrapped both arms around his leg. The child had been with a trusted babysitter for two hours. He was safe, fed, and smiling. Daniel still felt trapped.

"Let go. Daddy has bags."

The child held tighter. One bag split and oranges rolled under the table. Daniel's voice changed. "I said let go."

His son froze. Daniel saw fear on the small face and immediately felt ashamed. He had not meant to be frightening. He had meant to bring groceries inside.

Later, he noticed that the hardest part had not been the oranges. It had been the physical claim on him. In Daniel's childhood, needing another person was treated as weakness. Affection was available when it was convenient, and irritation followed quickly when it was not. His son's clinginess had touched that old rule before Daniel could name it.

The principle of this chapter is simple: ordinary child dependency can feel dangerous when your earlier safety depended on having few needs. The reaction may look like annoyance, urgency, numbness, or a wish to escape. None of those reactions tells you what your child deserves. They tell you where your system expects trouble.

The Hidden Rules About Need

Children ask for more than tasks. They ask to be carried, watched, reassured, answered, listened to, and helped with things they could sometimes do alone. They repeat questions. They want closeness at the moment the adult wants space. They become less capable when tired, sick, embarrassed, or in transition.

A parent who was welcomed in those states may still become overwhelmed. A parent who was shamed for them can experience an additional layer. The child's dependency can sound like a demand that has no end.

The old rule may be, "If I respond, I will disappear."

It may be, "If I do not fix this, I am failing."

It may be, "People who need too much are unsafe."

These rules are often contradictory. A parent can feel compelled to solve everything and resentful that anyone needs help. The contradiction makes sense when both strategies once protected connection. Being useful earned approval. Having needs risked rejection.

The first task is not to erase the rule. It is to recognize it as an old instruction rather than a current fact.

Activation Is Fast

Parental self-regulation is linked to how parents respond to, express, and discuss emotion with children, although the research is complex and does not reduce parenting to one trait (Edler & Valentino, 2024). In daily life, this means your capacity can change from one hour to the next. A cry that feels manageable after lunch may feel unbearable at the end of a long shift. The same child behavior can land differently when you are rested, rushed, touched out, worried about money, or in conflict with a partner.

This is useful because it moves you away from the question, "Why am I like this?" and toward a better one: "What increased the load in this moment?"

Look for body signals before you look for a perfect explanation. Your jaw tightens. Your breath becomes shallow. You start moving faster. You repeat yourself. You hear contempt in your inner voice. You stop being curious.

Those are not proof that damage has occurred. They are early warnings that choice is narrowing.

A small intervention can happen at that point. Put the bags down. Turn off the stove. Sit on the floor. Use fewer words. Say, "I need one minute, and I am staying nearby." The action should reduce pressure, not win the interaction.

Need Is Not the Same as Demand

Emotional neglect often leaves adults with two unhelpful categories: self-sufficient or demanding. Children do not fit neatly into either one.

A child can need reassurance and still hear no.

A child can be disappointed and still follow the plan.

A child can want your body close when your body needs space.

Your job is not to prove that the need is reasonable before responding. Your job is to identify what kind of response is possible and appropriate.

Consider a five-year-old who asks you to lie beside the bed until sleep. The child's wish for closeness is real. Your need for rest or time with another child is also real. You might say, "You want me to stay all night. I can sit for five minutes, then I will check once after you are tucked in."

That sentence does three things. It sees the wish, states the limit, and offers a reliable form of connection. It does not require either person to disappear.

The Cost of Calling It Manipulation

Parents sometimes use the word manipulation when a child discovers that behavior affects adults. Young children cry harder when a caregiver moves away. School-age children negotiate. Teenagers choose the argument most likely to reach the parent's weak spot.

Behavior can be strategic without being sinister. A child may be trying to prevent separation, avoid shame, gain control, or get relief. The strategy can still be unacceptable. The interpretation matters because it changes the adult's posture.

If you think, "She is trying to control me," you are more likely to enter a contest.

If you think, "She is trying to change an outcome she dislikes," you can stay in charge without treating the child as an enemy.

Try language that describes function rather than character: "You keep asking because you hope my answer will change. The answer is still no." This is firmer than a lecture about manipulation because it addresses what is happening and closes the negotiation.

Capacity Comes Before Character

A child who falls apart after school may have held it together for hours. A toddler who refuses shoes may be hungry. A teenager who snaps may be embarrassed. None of these possibilities excuses cruelty, aggression, or unsafe behavior. They help you decide what intervention has a chance of working.

When parents were expected to function beyond their developmental capacity, they may apply the same standard without noticing. A seven-year-old forgets the water bottle, and the parent hears irresponsibility. A 13-year-old needs help starting a project, and the parent hears laziness. The parent's history can turn a skill gap into a moral judgment.

Ask three questions before assigning character:

> *Does my child know how to do this?*

Can my child do it under current conditions?

What support would help without taking over?

The answers can lead to teaching, a checklist, a consequence, or a limit. They usually lead somewhere more useful than shame.

Try It: The Need Map

Choose one recurring moment that reliably irritates you. Write the child's visible behavior in neutral language. Replace "whines for attention" with "uses a high voice and asks me to watch repeatedly." Replace "acts helpless" with "asks me to begin the task with him."

Then complete four sentences:

> *My child may be seeking...*

The old rule this wakes in me is...

The limit or capacity issue is...

The smallest responsive action I can offer is...

For Daniel, the map looked like this:

> *His child was seeking reconnection after separation.*

The old rule was that physical need would take over.

The capacity issue was that Daniel's hands were full and his body felt crowded.

The responsive action was to put the bags down, offer a 20-second hug, then say, "You can walk beside me while I bring these in."

The goal was not to enjoy being grabbed. It was to respond to the need without letting activation choose the tone.

What to Remember About Need

A child's dependency can press directly on the part of you that survived by not depending. That reaction deserves attention, but it does not deserve command.

Need is information. It is not automatically an emergency, a moral failure, or an attempt to erase you.

You can acknowledge a wish without fulfilling it completely. You can protect your body without punishing the child for reaching. You can offer less than the child wants and still offer something reliable.

The first cycle-breaking move is often modest: stop treating your activation as proof that the child is too much.

Chapter 2: Separate Then from Now

Priya's eight-year-old had forgotten the permission slip again. The school trip was the next morning. Priya found the paper under a pile of drawings and felt an instant rush of panic.

"You never keep track of anything," she said. "Do you understand what happens when people cannot depend on you?"

Her son stared at the floor. Priya heard the size of her own sentence. A missed form had become a lesson about whether a person could be trusted.

The old story was not about the school trip. Priya had spent childhood monitoring adults who forgot appointments, bills, and promises. Competence had become her route to safety. Her son's ordinary disorganization felt like the beginning of chaos.

The central principle is the Two-Story Pause: in a charged moment, separate the child's present story from the rule your past is trying to enforce. Both stories can be real. Only one belongs in the driver's seat.

Story One Is the Present

Begin with observable facts. What happened without interpretation?

The form was not returned.

The milk spilled.

The child shouted, "I hate you."

The teenager came home 20 minutes late.

Facts keep the problem sized correctly. Interpretation can expand it into disrespect, ingratitude, danger, or proof of future failure before you know what happened.

Next, ask what developmental, emotional, or practical factors might be relevant. This is not an excuse hunt. It is an attempt to understand the task.

A child may need a visual reminder rather than another speech.

A teenager may need a consequence and a chance to explain.

A preschooler may not have the capacity to stop crying on command.

The ability to think about behavior in terms of underlying thoughts, feelings, and intentions is often described as parental reflective functioning. Reviews link stronger reflective capacity with more sensitive and responsive caregiving, while also noting that context, stress, and measurement matter (Camoirano, 2017; Huynh et al., 2024). In plain language, curiosity gives you more options than certainty.

Story Two Is the Old Rule

The old story is rarely a complete memory. It is more often a conclusion.

Mistakes lead to humiliation.

Anger destroys relationships.

No one will help, so I must control everything.

If a child is upset, the parent has failed.

My body belongs to whoever needs it.

Strong feelings should end quickly.

Your old rule can have helped you anticipate the adults around you. It can have earned praise. It can have prevented punishment. Respecting its original purpose can make it easier to loosen.

Try saying internally, "This rule helped me once. I am checking whether it fits now."

That sentence is different from arguing with yourself. You do not need to prove the rule foolish. You need to update its jurisdiction.

The Four Questions

The Two-Story Pause uses four questions. They can be written on a card, stored in your phone, or practiced after the event until they become familiar.

First: What is happening in the room right now?

Describe the behavior, the immediate risk, and the practical task. Priya's answer was, "The form is unsigned, the deadline is tomorrow, and my son is ashamed."

Second: What old rule or fear has awakened in me?

Priya's answer was, "If I do not force competence, everything will become chaotic."

Third: What does my child need from the adult in this moment?

The answer was not rescue from every consequence. It was help solving the immediate problem without turning forgetfulness into a character verdict.

Fourth: What is the smallest steady action I can take next?

Priya signed the form, put it by the backpack, and said, "We need a system because reminders are not working. We will make one after dinner." Later, she apologized for saying he was undependable.

The pause did not erase the problem. It removed the extra injury.

When the Old Story Is Partly Right

Some parents become afraid that any reference to the past will make them doubt sound judgment. That is not the purpose.

A child can be unsafe.

A teenager can lie.

A family can need a firm rule.

A parent's alarm can contain valid information.

The question is not, "Is this only a trigger?" The question is, "How much of my reaction belongs to the present, and what response fits the actual risk?"

Suppose your 14-year-old arrives home smelling of alcohol. The present story requires safety assessment, direct questions, supervision, and possibly medical help. It does not require insults, threats of abandonment, or turning the event into proof that the teenager is ruined. Separating stories makes action more precise, not less serious.

Avoid the Courtroom

Activation often turns a family conversation into a trial. The parent gathers old evidence, argues intent, and seeks a confession.

"You knew exactly what you were doing."

"You always make everything harder."

"Admit that you do not care."

Courtroom language feels powerful because it promises certainty. It rarely produces useful information. Children defend themselves, collapse, or say whatever ends the interrogation.

Use investigator language instead:

> *"Tell me what happened from the beginning."*

"What did you think would happen next?"

"What part is hard to say?"

"What needs to be made right?"

Investigator language does not remove accountability. It improves the quality of the evidence on which accountability rests.

Do Not Hand the Child Your Past

There is a difference between honest context and emotional burden.

A parent can say, "Loud voices are hard for me, so I am going to lower mine and ask you to lower yours."

A parent should be cautious about saying, "You sound exactly like the person who hurt me."

The first statement gives useful information and models responsibility. The second asks the child to manage an adult association they did not create.

Children can know that parents have histories and feelings. They should not become the container for those histories during conflict.

Process the old story with another adult, in writing, or with a qualified professional. Give the child only the information that helps the present relationship.

On Paper: The Two Columns

Draw a line down a page. Label the left side "Now" and the right side "Then."

Under Now, write only what could have been recorded by a camera, plus the immediate safety or practical issue.

Under Then, write the rule, fear, body memory, or expected consequence that appeared.

Finish with one sentence: "Because this is now, I can..."

Examples:

> *Because this is now, I can let my child be disappointed without withdrawing love.*

Because this is now, I can ask for help instead of controlling every detail.

Because this is now, I can stop the hitting without shaming the anger.

Because this is now, I can make a plan after my body settles.

This exercise is especially useful after an incident. Retrospective practice is not second rate. It is how the mind learns to recognize the pattern earlier next time.

Keep the Stories Separate

Respond to the problem that is actually in front of you, at the size it has now.

Your old story may explain the intensity of your reaction, but it does not decide what happens next.

Curiosity is not permissiveness. It is disciplined uncertainty. It keeps you from mistaking your first interpretation for the whole child.

When you separate then from now, you do not deny the past. You stop requiring the present family to reenact it.

Chapter 3: Build a Usable Pause

Regulation is not a mood a parent must achieve before parenting. It is the ability to create enough space between impulse and action to choose what happens next.

Marcus believed that calm parents spoke softly. On difficult mornings he could not speak softly, so he assumed the skill was unavailable.

His six-year-old moved at the speed of wet cement before school. Marcus repeated instructions, checked the clock, and felt his chest tighten. By the time the shoe was missing, calm was gone.

One morning he tried something smaller. He stopped talking, put both hands on the counter, and exhaled once. Then he said, “We have five minutes. I will find the shoe. You put on the coat.”

He was not peaceful. His voice was not warm. It was steady enough.

Marcus’s pause was physical, brief, and imperfect. That is what made it usable.

Drop the Calmness Test

The instruction to “stay calm” can become another standard used against parents. It suggests that if your heart is racing, you have already failed.

Children do benefit from adults who can provide containment. That does not require an adult to feel serene. It requires the adult to avoid making the child responsible for the adult’s internal storm.

Enough steadiness can look like:

> *Lowering the volume by one level.*

Using one sentence instead of six.

Moving an unsafe object out of reach.

Saying, “I need 30 seconds before I answer.”

Calling another caregiver to take over.

Postponing a lecture until everyone can think.

The body can remain activated while behavior becomes more intentional. That distinction is hopeful because behavior is often the first place change becomes visible.

Catch the Narrowing

Activation narrows attention. You stop seeing context and start seeing threat. The child becomes "disrespectful" rather than tired, "controlling" rather than scared, "lazy" rather than overwhelmed.

Create a personal list of narrowing signs. Common signs include speed, repetition, sarcasm, a desire to force eye contact, a sudden need to settle the entire issue now, or a fantasy of walking away for a long time.

Marcus's earliest sign was repeating the same instruction with more words. He began to use repetition as a cue: if he had said it twice, he stopped and changed the environment.

He might point to the checklist, bring the backpack to the door, or assign one task at a time. The cue did not make mornings pleasant. It prevented escalation from becoming the organizing method.

Use the Body First

When the thinking mind is crowded, physical actions are easier to retrieve than insight.

Plant both feet.

Unclench your hands.

Step back far enough to see the child's whole body.

Drop your shoulders.

Take a longer exhale.

Drink water.

Turn your face away briefly if eye contact is increasing intensity.

These actions are not magic switches. They are ways to signal that you are not required to act at the speed of the alarm.

Be cautious with practices that make you more distressed. Some people find closing their eyes, focusing intensely on breath, or scanning the body uncomfortable. Choose a method that increases orientation to the room rather than forcing an internal state.

Make the Environment Help

Self-regulation is not only an inner skill. Families can reduce predictable pressure.

If departures are explosive, create a launch area for shoes, bags, and forms.

If dinner preparation collides with a child's need for connection, build a brief reunion ritual before cooking.

If bedtime becomes a negotiation, make the sequence visible and decide in advance where flexibility ends.

If noise pushes you toward shutdown, use ear protection that lowers volume while allowing you to supervise and hear speech.

Environmental support is not cheating. It is good design. Parents who grew up overfunctioning may believe they should be able to manage without systems. Systems protect relationships from preventable strain.

Use the Pause Script

Prepare a sentence for moments when you cannot yet respond well.

"I hear you. I need a minute to think."

"I am too upset to answer carefully. I will come back in five minutes."

"I will not let anyone hit. We are moving apart."

"This matters. We are not solving it while we are yelling."

"I am staying nearby, and I am not talking yet."

A useful pause script includes connection, a limit when needed, and a return. Avoid vague departures such as "I cannot deal with you." The child hears rejection and does not know when the adult will reappear.

The return matters. If you say five minutes, come back in roughly five minutes. If you need longer, update the child: "I need 10 more minutes. You are safe. We will talk after the timer."

When You Cannot Leave

Parents often receive advice to take a break when the situation makes that impossible. A toddler cannot be left near water. A child in a parking lot needs immediate supervision. A teenager may be blocking a door. Safety comes first.

Use a micro-pause. Reduce words. Move bodies to safety. Repeat one line.

"I will not let you run into the street."

"You are safe. I am holding your hand."

"We will talk when we are in the car."

Do not use the dangerous setting to teach the entire lesson. Contain first. Explain later.

Build Recovery Into the Day

A nervous system asked to absorb repeated stress without recovery becomes less flexible. Parents with histories of neglect may treat recovery as something earned after all tasks are complete. In family life, tasks are rarely complete.

Recovery can be three minutes in the parked car, a quiet shower, a short walk, music through one earbud while preparing lunch, a text to a supportive friend, or a handoff arranged before resentment peaks.

The important question is not whether the activity qualifies as ideal self-care. It is whether it returns some capacity.

Also examine structural burdens. No breathing technique can replace sleep indefinitely, make unsafe housing safe, resolve financial pressure, or provide childcare. Personal skills matter, and so do resources, schedules, labor distribution, and community support.

In the Moment: The Ten Percent Shift

Choose one recurring situation. Do not aim to feel calm. Aim to make the response 10 percent less automatic.

Write:

> *My first body signal is...*

My usual automatic move is...

My 10 percent shift will be...

My return sentence will be...

Marcus wrote that his first signal was rapid speech. His automatic move was stacking instructions. His shift was to stop after one instruction and point to the morning card. His return sentence was, "We were both rushed. Tonight we will put the shoes by the door."

A 10 percent shift is deliberately modest. Repetition turns modest changes into available habits.

A Pause You Can Use

You do not need to feel peaceful to act with care.

A pause is not avoidance when it protects the relationship and includes a return.

Use the body, the room, and the schedule. Regulation is not a private test of character.

The best pause is the one you can remember when the morning is already going wrong.

Chapter 4: See Before You Solve

When a child brings home pain, adults often reach for the quickest available tool: explanation. Facts, reassurance, perspective, and plans can all be useful. Used too early, they can sound like instructions to stop feeling.

Lena's 10-year-old came home after a friendship conflict and said she was never going back to school. Lena immediately began solving.

"You have other friends."

"You cannot avoid school."

"Maybe you misunderstood."

"Tell the teacher tomorrow."

Her daughter stopped talking. Lena had offered facts, perspective, and a plan. None of it reached the child.

Later, Lena tried again. "It sounds like lunch felt humiliating."

Her daughter nodded and began to describe what had happened. The conversation did not repair the friendship or make school easy the next morning. It did give them accurate information: the child felt publicly excluded, and the school needed to know.

The principle is not that solutions are bad. It is that a child often needs evidence of being understood before advice can be used. Seeing is a form of orientation: you identify the emotional weather before deciding what equipment is needed.

Notice Without Interrogating

Parents who grew up with little emotional attention may swing between missing cues and investigating them intensely. A child looks upset, and the parent asks six questions in 30 seconds.

"What happened?"

"Who did it?"

"Why did you not tell the teacher?"

"Are you being bullied?"

The urgency can make the child feel watched rather than seen.

Start with an observation and an opening.

"You got quiet when I mentioned practice."

"You came in and went straight to your room."

"Your face changed when that message arrived."

"I am available if you want to tell me."

The observation says you noticed. The opening leaves room for consent and timing.

Name With Humility

Emotion words can help children organize experience, especially when they are offered as possibilities rather than verdicts. The adult might say, "You seem disappointed," or "I wonder if that felt embarrassing."

Use tentative language because you can be wrong. A child who looks angry may be scared. A teenager who seems indifferent may be protecting privacy. The goal is not to prove your emotional accuracy. It is to make inner experience discussable.

If the child says, "No, I am not embarrassed," resist arguing.

Try, "Okay. What word fits better?"

Or, "You do not have to name it. I can see it mattered."

Being corrected is not failure. It teaches the child that their inner experience belongs to them.

Do Not Rush the Silver Lining

Some adults learned that difficult feelings were tolerated only if converted quickly into gratitude, resilience, or a lesson.

"At least you were invited."

"Everything happens for a reason."

"You will laugh about this later."

A wider perspective can be helpful after the feeling has been met. Too early, it communicates that the emotion must leave before connection can begin.

Try sequence instead:

> *First, "That was a painful thing to hear."*

Then, after space, "Do you want help thinking about tomorrow?"

The sequence respects time. It also reduces the parent's impulse to make the child feel better so the parent can feel better.

See the Need Under the Behavior

Emotionally seeing a child does not mean accepting the behavior at face value. It means asking what the behavior is trying to accomplish.

A child who boasts may be seeking status after feeling small.

A child who refuses help may be protecting competence.

A child who argues every detail may be trying to regain control.

A child who jokes during a serious conversation may be avoiding shame.

You can respond to the need while limiting the strategy.

"You want me to know you are capable. I will let you try, and I am staying close."

"You want more control. You can choose the order, but both tasks need to be done."

"You are trying to make this less uncomfortable by joking. We still need to finish the conversation."

This is not mind reading. Offer your interpretation lightly and watch what happens.

Use Attention Before Correction

Responsive interaction is built through repeated back-and-forth exchanges, not only through formal talks. Young children point, babble, show objects, ask the same question, and watch whether an adult returns attention. The Center on the Developing Child at Harvard University emphasizes that these responsive exchanges support early social and communication development (Center on the Developing Child at Harvard University, n.d.).

For older children, the form changes but the principle remains useful. They send a clip, tell a long story about a game, complain about a teacher, or hover in the kitchen. The content may seem trivial. The bid for attention may not be.

You cannot respond to every bid. No parent can. Look for small returns:

> *"Show me the best part."*

"I cannot watch now. Save it for after dinner."

"You have 60 seconds. Give me the headline."

"I want to hear this when I can listen. Come back at eight."

A reliable delayed response is often more connecting than distracted half-attention.

When the Child Does Not Want to Talk

Some children process privately. Some need movement, parallel activity, or time. Some become less communicative when adults make direct eye contact.

Try talking in the car, while walking, folding laundry, drawing, or doing a task side by side. Ask one question and leave space.

Respecting privacy is not the same as ignoring warning signs. If you notice a marked change in sleep, eating, school functioning, relationships, safety, or mood, seek appropriate guidance even if the child resists discussion. Chapter 15 addresses this more fully.

For ordinary reluctance, communicate availability without pressure: "You do not have to talk now. I will check again tonight."

Then check again.

When Listening Does Not Solve the Problem

Some problems remain after a child feels heard. A friendship may still be unsafe, a teacher may need to intervene, a consequence may still be necessary, or the child may still refuse the next step.

Do not turn listening into a promise that you will stay passive. Say what you understand, then state the adult action that is required: "I believe you did not want anyone involved. Because the messages include threats, I am going to contact the school."

Being emotionally seen means the child does not have to manage the problem alone. It does not mean the child controls every decision about safety.

Listening Practice: The Ninety-Second Listen

Once this week, when your child brings a nonemergency problem, listen for 90 seconds before offering advice.

During that time, use only three kinds of responses:

> *A neutral observation: "That changed fast."*

A feeling possibility: "You sound disappointed."

An invitation: "What happened next?"

At the end, ask, "Do you want listening, ideas, or help taking action?"

Children may not know. You can offer choices: "I can sit with you, help draft a message, or give you space."

The exercise is not about a stopwatch. It is about discovering how quickly the adult usually moves from contact to correction.

See Before Solving

Begin by understanding what the child experienced; that information changes which solution, if any, will fit.

Name emotion with humility. Let the child correct you.

Do not make optimism the admission price for comfort.

Attention is not unlimited, but it can be honest. A clear later is kinder than a distracted now.

When a child feels accurately seen, guidance has somewhere to land.

Chapter 5: Validate Without Giving In

Validation is often confused with agreement, permission, or surrender. That confusion becomes strongest when a child is exaggerating, accusing, or demanding something the adult has already refused.

Sofia's seven-year-old wanted a second cookie before dinner. When Sofia said no, he shouted, "You never let me have anything."

Sofia had read that she should validate feelings. She worried that saying, "That is hard," would reward the outburst. She also worried that holding the limit would repeat the emotional coldness of her childhood.

She tried, "You really wanted another cookie, and you are angry that the answer is no. Dinner is in 20 minutes."

Her son remained angry. He complained through dinner and brought it up again the next day. The limit remained, and Sofia did not turn the disagreement into a fight about whether he was allowed to feel it.

The principle is that validation and agreement are different acts. Validation identifies an understandable inner experience. It does not declare the child's interpretation accurate, remove consequences, or approve harmful behavior.

What Validation Actually Does

Validation says, "I can see how this makes sense from where you are standing."

It can acknowledge emotion: "You are furious."

It can acknowledge desire: "You wanted more time."

It can acknowledge meaning: "It felt like I chose your brother."

It can acknowledge effort: "You worked hard and the result was disappointing."

AAP guidance for caregivers makes the same distinction in practical terms: a parent can validate a child's emotion without agreeing with everything the child says or does (Pianka, 2025).

Validation is not a technique for making feelings disappear. The child may stay disappointed. In fact, a parent who expects validation to stop the emotion can become frustrated when it works only as recognition.

The listening is working when the child experiences contact rather than an attempt to steer the answer.

The Three-Part Response

A reliable response has three parts:

> *Name the experience.*

State the boundary or reality.

Offer the next available form of support.

For a toddler: "You want the knife. It is not safe. You can hold the wooden spoon."

For a school-age child: "You hate that screen time is over. The tablet is charging in my room. You can choose music or drawing."

For a teenager: "You feel excluded by the rule. Curfew is still 11. I will pick you up, or you can arrange a ride with Maya's parent."

The order matters. Starting with the boundary can make the child fight to prove the feeling. Starting with the feeling makes it easier to hear the limit, though it does not guarantee cooperation.

Validate the Feeling Not the Distortion

Children make global statements under stress.

"No one likes me."

"You always choose her."

"I am terrible at everything."

You do not need to confirm the distortion to validate the pain.

Instead of, "Yes, everyone was cruel," say, "You felt left out when no one saved a seat."

Instead of, "I do always choose your sister," say, "It looked that way when I went to her game and missed yours."

Instead of arguing, "You are good at lots of things," say, "That mistake made you feel like giving up."

Specific language holds emotion without strengthening an inaccurate conclusion.

Validation Does Not Excuse Harm

A child can have a valid feeling and an unacceptable action.

"You were angry. You may not call her that."

"You wanted the toy. You may not grab."

"You felt trapped. Punching the wall is not safe."

Parents who were punished for emotion may confuse limits on behavior with rejection of emotion. Keep them separate in language and action. Stop the harmful behavior firmly. Avoid contempt, threats of emotional abandonment, or demands that the child stop feeling before returning to connection.

The child may need to make amends after settling. Validation does not cancel repair. It makes accountability less dependent on shame.

When Validation Sounds Fake

Children can hear a script delivered through clenched teeth. If the polished sentence feels false, simplify.

"You are mad. The answer is no."

"I hear that you hate this. We are still leaving."

"That hurt. I am not ready to discuss the decision yet."

Warmth is helpful. Honesty is essential. A brief true sentence is better than an elaborate performance.

Also notice repeated use of "I understand" when you do not. Try, "I want to understand," or "I can see that this matters." These phrases leave room for difference.

Do Not Debate During the Peak

When a child is highly activated, long explanations can add pressure. The parent may keep talking because silence feels like failure.

Use one validation line and one limit line. Then reduce language.

"You are angry that we are leaving. We are leaving now."

Repeat if necessary. Do not add new reasons each time. New reasons become new openings for argument.

Later, when both people can think, discuss the pattern, hear the child's view, and decide whether the rule needs adjustment. A limit held during a meltdown is not the final word on family policy.

Cultural and Family Language

Families differ in how directly they name emotion, how much eye contact they use, and how they express respect. Emotional responsiveness does not require every household to sound the same.

The core questions are broader:

> *Can the child show distress without being mocked or threatened?*

Can the adult hold authority without denying the child's inner experience?

Can the family return after conflict?

Can emotion be discussed in language that fits the family?

A grandparent may say, "I know your heart is heavy," while another caregiver says, "You seem sad." The wording differs. The act of recognition is similar.

A Four-Step Exercise: The Validation Ladder

Take a recent conflict and write four versions of a response.

Level one, observation: "You slammed the book shut."

Level two, emotion possibility: "You seem frustrated."

Level three, meaning: "It feels unfair to work this hard and still miss the answer."

Level four, boundary and support: "We are not throwing the book. We can take five minutes, then decide whether you want help."

You do not need all four levels in every moment. The ladder teaches you to move from visible behavior toward inner experience without losing the limit.

Validation in Practice

Validation is not permission. It is recognition.

A feeling can make sense while a behavior remains unacceptable.

Specific language is safer than agreeing with global statements.

You do not have to remove disappointment to remain connected.

The strongest boundary often sounds like two truths held together: "I see why you want it, and the answer is still no."

Chapter 6: Hold Limits, Stay Connected

Aisha's five-year-old wanted to keep building when it was time to leave the library. Aisha gave a five-minute warning, then a two-minute warning. When she said it was time, he swept the blocks onto the floor.

Aisha felt two impulses at once. One was to go cold and make him feel the seriousness of what he had done. The other was to give him more time so he would not experience the kind of harsh ending she remembered from childhood.

She chose a third response.

"I will not let you throw the blocks. We are cleaning three together, then we are leaving. You can be angry with me."

Her son cried while they cleaned. Aisha stayed close. The limit was not pleasant, but it did not require emotional exile.

The principle is that structure and connection are not opposites. A boundary tells the child what will happen. Connection tells the child that the relationship remains available while it happens.

A Limit Is Not a Punishment

A limit is the line that protects safety, time, property, bodies, or family functioning.

A punishment adds suffering in order to make the child regret the behavior.

The difference can become blurred. Leaving the library because it is closing is a limit. Refusing to speak to the child for the ride home is an added disconnection. Removing a toy used to hit is a safety response. Throwing away unrelated toys to "teach a lesson" is escalation.

Parents who experienced emotional withdrawal may reproduce it because silence feels more controlled than shouting. The child still experiences uncertainty: Is the relationship gone? How long will this last? What must I do to bring the adult back?

You can take space without using absence as leverage. Say what is happening and when you will return.

"I am too angry to talk kindly. I will sit in the kitchen for five minutes. You are safe, and we will finish this."

Make the Limit Concrete

Vague commands invite confusion.

"Be respectful."

"Act your age."

"Stop being difficult."

Concrete limits describe behavior and next action.

"Keep your hands on your own body."

"You may disagree without calling names."

"The game is finished for today because the controller was thrown."

"We are leaving at six. You may walk or I will help you."

A concrete limit also lets the parent know when the task is complete. "Be respectful" has no clear finish. "Use a voice that does not hurt ears" is observable.

Use Fewer Reasons

Parents who were not given explanations may overcorrect by explaining every rule at length. Explanations are respectful when the child can receive them. During resistance, too many reasons can sound like negotiation.

State the reason once.

"The stove is hot, so you cannot touch the pan."

Then hold the line.

If the child keeps arguing, use a closed response: "I hear that you disagree. The answer is not changing."

Explanations belong to teaching. Repetition belongs to containment. Know which job you are doing.

Hold the Child's Feeling and Your Decision

A connected limit often includes four elements:

> *Acknowledge the wish.*

State the decision.

Allow the feeling.

Protect the boundary.

"You wanted to stay. We are leaving. You can be disappointed. I will help your body move if you cannot walk."

This is not a script for every age. With a teenager it may sound like, "You think the rule is unfair. Curfew stays at 11 tonight. We can review it this weekend. If you are not home, you lose driving privileges tomorrow."

The emotional message is consistent: disagreement does not cancel authority, and authority does not cancel relationship.

When the Child Escalates

Some children escalate because the limit is new. Some because the limit removes something regulating or rewarding. Some because they are exhausted, anxious, impulsive, or developmentally unable to shift quickly.

An escalation does not automatically mean the limit was wrong.

Check three things:

> *Is the limit necessary?*

Is the expectation within the child's capacity?

Can I reduce stimulation while holding it?

You may lower your voice, remove an audience, give two acceptable choices, or wait before discussing consequences. Do not add threats because the child is showing distress. Add action only when safety requires it.

When the Limit Is Tested Again

A connected limit is often tested more than once. Repetition does not prove that the wording failed or that the child is deliberately trying to defeat you. The child may be checking whether the boundary is real, whether the relationship survives it, or whether a different strategy will change the answer.

Keep the core boundary stable and change only what improves capacity: the warning, the environment, the number of words, the transition support, or the timing of the discussion. A limit becomes predictable through repetition, not through one perfectly handled scene.

Natural and Related Consequences

A useful consequence is related, proportionate, and understandable.

If markers are used on the wall, markers move to supervised use.

If a teenager misses the agreed pickup without contact, the next outing requires a clearer transportation plan.

If a child breaks a sibling's item in anger, repair can include helping replace or fix it.

Avoid unrelated penalties that make the adult feel powerful but teach little. Losing a birthday party because homework was forgotten may create resentment without building the missing planning skill.

Consequences work best when paired with instruction. Ask, "What skill would make this less likely next time?" The answer may be a reminder, a transition warning, practice asking for help, or a plan for leaving before overload.

Boundaries for the Parent's Body

Cycle-breaking parents sometimes believe they must accept unwanted touch to prove warmth. You are allowed to protect your body.

"I am not available for climbing right now. You can sit beside me."

"I will hug you for 10 seconds, then I need space."

"You may be angry. You may not follow me into the bathroom."

A body boundary is not emotional rejection when it is clear and respectful. It teaches children that closeness includes consent.

Offer another form of connection when possible. A child who cannot be on your lap may hold your hand, lean against a pillow beside you, or choose a book to read later.

Plan It: The Connected Limit

Choose one limit you repeat often. Write it in three lines:

> *The experience: "You want..."*

The boundary: "I will not..." or "We are..."

The connection: "I can..." or "I will stay..."

Example:

> *"You want to keep playing."*

"We are turning the game off at seven."

"I will sit with you while you save, and you can choose what we do for the next 10 minutes."

Practice the words before the situation. Familiar language is easier to retrieve under stress.

Connected Limits

A limit protects. It does not need to wound in order to count.

Connection does not mean changing the answer. It means the child does not have to earn the relationship back after being disappointed.

Use concrete language, fewer reasons, and related consequences.

You can be firm without becoming cold. In many families, that is the new pattern the child will remember.

Chapter 7: Meet Tears and Clinginess

At drop-off, tears provide information but not a verdict. By themselves, they do not tell you whether separation is harmful, whether the child should stay home, or whether the adult has handled the morning badly.

Ben's daughter started kindergarten confidently. Three weeks later she began crying at drop-off and asking to sleep in his room. Ben felt embarrassed by how quickly irritation appeared.

He had been praised throughout childhood for being independent. No one had asked whether the independence was chosen. Now his daughter's need for reassurance felt like regression, and regression felt dangerous.

One morning he knelt by the classroom door and said, "Part of you wants to stay with me. Your teacher will help you, and I will be back after snack and story time." He gave one hug, followed the agreed handoff, and left.

His daughter still cried. Some mornings she was building with blocks within 10 minutes. On others she cried through circle time and needed extra help from the teacher. Ben kept the goodbye brief, watched the pattern across several weeks, and remained willing to change the plan if the distress began to interfere with school or sleep.

The principle is that tears and clinginess are signals, not verdicts. They may reflect fatigue, transition, temperament, stress, fear, or a temporary drop in capacity. Your task is to respond to the signal while preserving the child's confidence in separation and return.

Why Dependency Can Feel Personal

A crying child can trigger beliefs about the parent.

I am doing something wrong.

I have made the child weak.

I am being controlled.

I will never get space again.

These beliefs turn the child's state into an evaluation of the adult. That raises urgency. The parent may overreassure, snap, or push independence before the child is ready.

Separate the questions.

What is my child communicating?

What level of support fits?

What is the plan for return?

You do not need the child to stop crying to know the plan is sound.

Reassurance Needs Structure

Reassurance without structure can grow into repeated checking.

"Are you sure you will come back?"

"Yes."

"Promise?"

"I promise."

"What if you forget?"

"I would never forget."

The loop continues because each answer briefly lowers distress without helping the child tolerate uncertainty.

Try a brief, consistent response tied to a concrete sequence.

"I will come back after music."

"Grandpa will stay while I am gone."

"The plan has not changed."

Then move toward the next action. Reassurance should support the plan, not replace it.

Do Not Shame the Reach

Avoid phrases that make closeness a character flaw.

"Big kids do not cry."

"You are acting like a baby."

"Stop being so clingy."

Even when the parent is trying to encourage courage, shame adds a second problem. The child now has fear and embarrassment about having fear.

Use language that holds both dependence and growth.

"You wish I could stay. You can miss me and still go in."

"You want help. I will start with you, then you will do the next part."

"You are tired and want to be carried. I can carry you to the stairs, then you walk."

The message is not that the child can have unlimited access. It is that needing connection is not humiliating.

Distress Is Not Always Danger

A parent who experienced neglect can become highly alarmed by any sign of a child's pain. This can lead to rescuing the child from manageable frustration.

A child who cries when a friend says no is distressed. The child may not be unsafe.

A child who protests a homework limit is distressed. The limit may still be appropriate.

A child who misses a parent during an overnight visit is distressed. The child may be capable of staying.

Ask whether the situation is harmful, overwhelming, or merely uncomfortable. Those are different categories.

Managed discomfort gives children practice discovering that emotion rises and falls. The adult's presence can be steady without removing every challenge.

Build Predictable Separation

Young children often benefit from clear rituals.

Use the same short goodbye.

Name the return point in terms the child understands.

Do not disappear secretly to avoid tears.

Do not stretch the goodbye through repeated returns unless safety requires it.

Coordinate with the receiving adult.

For older children, predictability may involve knowing where you are, when you will check in, and who is available if a plan changes. The exact level of contact should fit age, temperament, and circumstance.

The goal is not to make separation emotionless. It is to make it reliable.

Respond to Nighttime Need

Nighttime can activate both child fear and parent deprivation. A parent who had to self-soothe early can feel angry that a child asks for water, company, or repeated checks.

Begin by clarifying the pattern. Is the child ill, frightened, adjusting to change, avoiding sleep, or seeking extra connection after a disconnected day? Is the routine too late? Is the parent inconsistent, sometimes staying for an hour and sometimes leaving abruptly?

Create a plan you can repeat.

"Two stories, one drink, one hug, then lights out."

"If you call once, I will check. After that, I will answer from the hall unless you are sick or unsafe."

"I will sit by the bed for three minutes and move the chair closer to the door each night."

A plan should be kind enough to sustain and firm enough to be predictable.

Watch for Changes That Need Attention

Clinginess can be developmentally common, especially around transitions. It can also signal a problem that deserves assessment.

Pay attention to intensity, duration, and impairment. Has the child stopped participating in school, sleep, play, or ordinary routines? Is there a sudden change after a frightening event, bullying, illness, loss, or family conflict? Are there physical symptoms, panic, or persistent distress?

The CDC notes that persistent or extreme fears, or worries that interfere with home, school, or play, are reasons to speak with a healthcare provider about evaluation (Centers for Disease Control and Prevention, 2026). You do not need to diagnose the cause before asking a pediatrician or qualified mental health professional for guidance.

Prepare: The Separation Plan

Write a plan for one recurring separation.

Before: What connection happens first?

During: Who is responsible, and what is the child told?

Goodbye: What exact words will you use?

Return: When and how will reconnection happen?

If the child protests, what sentence will you repeat?

Ben's sentence was, "You want me to stay. Ms. Alvarez has you. I will be back after snack and story time." He stopped adding new promises. The ritual became familiar to both of them.

Responding to Dependency

Crying does not prove that the plan is wrong.

Closeness is not a defect to remove. It is a need to guide toward increasing capacity.

Offer reassurance that supports a predictable plan.

Do not confuse manageable distress with harm, and do not ignore persistent impairment.

The child learns independence through repeated experiences of connection, separation, and return.

Chapter 8: Respond to Anger Safely

A slammed door, a raised voice, and a thrown object all involve anger, but they do not carry the same level of danger. Parents who grew up around explosive or forbidden anger can react to all three as though catastrophe has already begun.

Carmen's 11-year-old slammed the bedroom door after being told he could not go to a sleepover. The sound sent Carmen back to a childhood home where anger meant broken objects and hours of silence.

She opened the door immediately and shouted, "Do not ever slam a door in my house."

Her son shouted back. Carmen felt the old fear becoming authority.

She stepped into the hall and said, "I am going to try that again. The door cannot be slammed. You can close it and have space. We will talk in 15 minutes."

The anger remained on both sides. The room became safer.

The principle is that anger needs containment without humiliation. Children need to learn that anger is information and energy, not permission to threaten, destroy, or dominate. Parents need the same distinction.

Your History Changes the Volume

Anger can have been dangerous in your family. It may also have been forbidden. Either history can make a child's anger hard to tolerate.

If anger was explosive, you may read every raised voice as the start of catastrophe.

If anger was forbidden, you can experience disagreement as disrespect.

If you were the peacemaker, you may rush to end conflict before anyone understands it.

The first task is to locate the actual level of danger. A scowl is not a threat. A slammed door is not the same as a thrown chair. A threat of harm requires a different response from sarcasm.

Size the intervention to the behavior.

Stop Harm Before Teaching

When a child is hitting, kicking, throwing dangerous objects, driving recklessly, or threatening harm, safety comes first.

Use direct language.

"I will not let you hit."

"Put the object down."

"Move away from your sister."

"We are calling for help because this is not safe."

Do not demand insight during the peak. Do not corner a child physically unless immediate safety requires intervention and you are trained to do so. Increase distance, remove other children, reduce access to dangerous objects, and seek emergency assistance when there is imminent risk.

After safety is restored, teaching can begin.

Separate Anger From Aggression

Anger is an emotional state. Aggression is behavior intended or likely to cause harm.

A child may say, "I am furious," stomp, cry, ask for space, or write an angry note without being aggressive.

A child may also insult, threaten, hit, or destroy property. Those behaviors need limits and repair.

Use language that preserves the distinction:

> *"You may be angry. You may not scare people."*

"You may take space. You may not damage the door."

"You can tell me you hate the rule. You cannot use slurs."

This teaches that the goal is not emotional suppression. The goal is safe expression.

Give Anger a Job

Anger often points toward unfairness, blocked goals, shame, fear, or loss of control. Help the child identify the job without treating the feeling as a judge.

"What did the anger want to change?"

"What happened right before it got big?"

"What were you protecting?"

"What would a safe version of that message sound like?"

A teenager may discover that anger was protecting embarrassment. A younger child may say, "I wanted him to stop." The answer gives you material for skill building.

Practice replacement actions before the next event: step away, call an adult, use a set phrase, put hands in pockets, or request a break.

Keep Your Authority Out of the Fight

A parent's fear can turn conflict into a struggle over who has power.

"You will not speak to me that way."

"I am the parent."

"Do it because I said so."

Authority is real, but repeating status often means the adult has lost the practical objective.

Return to the issue.

"The sleepover answer is no because the supervision plan is unclear."

"The door needs to be used safely."

"We will speak without insults or pause the conversation."

The goal is not to defeat the child's anger. It is to keep the family safe and move toward accountability.

Repair After Aggression

When harm occurred, repair should address impact.

A complete repair can include acknowledging what happened, replacing or fixing property, checking on the person harmed, practicing an alternative, and accepting a related consequence.

Avoid forced apologies delivered under threat. They teach performance more than responsibility.

Ask, "What do you think your sister experienced?" If the child cannot answer, provide information without contempt: "She moved behind the couch and cried. Your throwing scared her."

Then ask, "What can you do now, and what will you do differently when anger rises again?"

Some children need time before they can participate. Accountability can be delayed without being abandoned.

Model Anger Without Threat

Parents do not need to hide all anger.

"I am angry that the agreement was ignored."

"My voice is getting loud, so I am pausing."

"I need space before I say something harmful."

"I am still upset, and I am ready to talk."

This shows that anger can be named, regulated, and revisited. It also prevents children from learning that calm language means the adult has no feelings.

Family Safety Plan: The Anger Plan

Create a family plan during a neutral time.

Name early signs: faster speech, clenched hands, pacing, hot face.

Choose safe exits: bedroom door closed gently, porch, bathroom, walk with permission, headphones.

Set nonnegotiables: no hitting, threats, blocking exits, dangerous driving, or destruction.

Decide how return happens: a timer, check-in, written note, or scheduled conversation.

Decide how repair happens when harm occurs.

Post the plan if helpful. The purpose is not to eliminate anger. It is to reduce improvisation when thinking is hardest.

Anger and Safety

Anger is not the same as aggression.

Safety comes before explanation.

Do not use shame to teach control. Shame often adds more heat or pushes anger underground.

Authority works best when it stays focused on the actual boundary.

A family becomes safer when people can say, "I am angry," without making someone else afraid.

Chapter 9: Guide Without Controlling

Guidance becomes difficult when a child is old enough to have a real preference but not yet old enough to carry every consequence alone. The adult must decide what is fixed, what is negotiable, and what the child is ready to learn through experience.

Luis's 13-year-old wanted to quit the school band halfway through the year. Luis heard himself preparing a speech about commitment, wasted money, and future regret.

In his childhood, adults made major decisions without explanation. He had promised himself that his children would have a voice. Yet when his son used that voice to choose something Luis disliked, freedom suddenly felt irresponsible.

Instead of deciding in the first conversation, Luis said, "I will not make you stay forever, and I will not let you quit tonight. We need to understand what changed and what commitments remain."

The principle is that leadership gives children real influence within limits that reflect age, safety, and family responsibility. Control seeks certainty. Guidance builds judgment.

The Control Trap

Control can look strict, but it can also look anxious and overinvolved.

The parent reminds repeatedly, checks every assignment, solves every friendship problem, tracks every mood, and prevents every consequence. The child can appear successful while depending on the adult to supply organization and confidence.

Parents with neglect histories can be especially vulnerable to overfunctioning. If no one helped them, they may believe good parenting means never letting a child struggle. If chaos surrounded them, control can feel like love.

Ask, "Am I helping my child do this, or am I making it unnecessary for my child to learn?"

The answer changes by age and circumstance. A six-year-old needs more direct support than a 16-year-old. A child with a disability may need accommodations that peers do not. Guidance is not a race toward independence.

Give Bounded Choice

Choice is useful when every option is acceptable.

"You can shower before or after homework."

"You may wear the coat or carry it. We are bringing it."

"You can tell the coach yourself, or we can write the message together."

Avoid false choice: "Do you want to go to school?" when attendance is required. False choices create conflict because the adult asks a question but rejects the answer.

Bounded choice communicates respect without surrendering the frame.

Let Experience Teach

Some lessons are safer and more effective when experience provides the feedback.

A forgotten lunch can lead to using the school option.

A late assignment may receive the teacher's consequence.

A poorly planned outing may end early.

Before stepping back, check safety, developmental capacity, and stakes. Do not use "natural consequences" to justify preventable harm, humiliation, or neglect. A child should not go without necessary medication to learn responsibility.

The parent remains available to reflect afterward.

"What happened?"

"What will you change?"

"What support would help without me doing it for you?"

Explain Values Without Demanding Agreement

Families need rules based on values.

"We tell the truth because trust depends on accurate information."

"We include everyone in cleanup because everyone uses the space."

"We do not post pictures of others without permission."

Children may disagree. Your authority does not depend on their immediate agreement.

Avoid turning values into labels. "We value honesty" is different from "You are a liar." The first names a standard. The second turns a behavior into identity.

Respect Privacy

Emotionally neglectful homes can have too little interest in a child or too little respect for boundaries. Cycle-breaking requires a middle path.

Young children need close supervision. Older children need increasing privacy in bodies, communication, thought, and relationships, while parents retain responsibility for safety.

Do not read messages, search belongings, or disclose private information casually unless there is a proportionate safety reason. When monitoring is necessary, be as transparent as possible.

"I am checking the phone because of the threat you received. I will look only at the relevant messages."

"I will knock before entering unless I believe someone is unsafe."

Privacy teaches dignity. It is not secrecy without limits.

Allow Different Preferences

A child is not a correction of the parent's childhood.

The parent who was denied sports may push athletics.

The parent who was forced to perform may avoid all pressure.

The parent who felt invisible may expect constant emotional openness.

Children need room to be different from the parent's imagined repair.

Ask whether the activity serves the child's development or the parent's unfinished story. You can encourage persistence without requiring the child to redeem your past.

Use Collaboration for Repeating Problems

Collaboration is not a family vote on every rule. It is a structured way to gather information and design a workable plan.

State the concern without accusation.

"Homework is starting at 10, and sleep is suffering."

Ask for the child's view.

"What is making it hard to begin?"

Name the adult's nonnegotiable.

"You need enough sleep and the work must be addressed."

Generate options together.

The plan may include a start time, phone location, support period, or conversation with the teacher. Set a review date. Plans need evidence, not endless debate.

Review: The Guidance Check

Choose one area where you may be overfunctioning.

Write:

> *What responsibility belongs to me?*

What responsibility is ready to move toward my child?

What support will remain?

What consequence can occur safely?

What will I do with my own discomfort while the child learns?

Luis decided his son would speak with the band director and finish the current concert. His son stayed angry for several days and completed it without enthusiasm. Afterward, he chose to leave the band. The outcome was not the choice Luis preferred, but the process required the teenager to speak, complete an existing commitment, and make a decision he could explain. Luis offered transportation and help preparing the conversation; he did not write the message or make the decision alone.

Guidance Without Control

Control reduces uncertainty for the adult. Guidance develops capacity in the child.

Offer choices only when every answer is acceptable.

Let safe consequences teach, then help the child reflect.

Respect grows when children have a voice, even when they do not have the final decision.

The aim is not obedience without thought. It is judgment that can function when the parent is not in the room.

Chapter 10: Repair After You Disconnect

Grace had shouted at her nine-year-old for spilling juice on the laptop. The laptop survived. Her daughter's face changed.

Ten minutes later Grace wanted to apologize, but shame made the words complicated. She began, "I am sorry, but you know I have told you not to put drinks there."

Her daughter looked away.

Grace stopped. "That was not an apology. I was scared about the computer, and I shouted in a way that scared you. The spill was a mistake. My shouting was my responsibility. I am sorry."

The child did not smile. She said, "Okay," and went back to drawing.

Repair does not always produce a warm scene. Its purpose is to restore truth, safety, and responsibility. The principle is not that good parents avoid every rupture. It is that they do not make the child carry the cost of the rupture or pretend it did not happen.

Rupture Is Part of Relationship

Research on parent-infant interaction describes relationships as patterns of coordination, mismatch, and repair rather than uninterrupted harmony. The practical lesson should be stated carefully: ordinary misattunement occurs, and returning to contact matters (Tronick & Beeghly, 2011).

This is not permission for repeated harm. A sincere apology cannot compensate for ongoing intimidation, violence, or emotional withdrawal without meaningful change and appropriate help.

For ordinary parenting failures, however, perfection is the wrong standard. A child can learn that people make mistakes, name impact, and work to restore trust.

The Five Parts of Repair

A useful repair includes five parts.

Name what you did.

Name the likely impact.

Take responsibility without a defense.

State what you will do differently.

Make room for the child's response.

"I yelled and called you selfish. That was hurtful and unfair. I was overwhelmed, but managing that was my job. Next time I will pause before I answer. You do not have to make me feel better. Is there anything you want me to understand?"

Keep the repair sized to the event. Do not turn a brief sharp tone into a long confession that asks the child to comfort you.

Remove the Hidden But

"I am sorry, but..." usually means the apology is still trying to win.

The child's behavior can be addressed separately.

First: "I am sorry I grabbed the controller. I should not have used force."

Later: "We still need to address the rule you broke."

Separating repair from discipline makes both clearer. The parent owns the adult behavior. The child remains accountable for the child behavior.

Repair After Withdrawal

Some parents do not shout. They disappear emotionally.

They answer with one word, avoid eye contact, become icy, or stay busy until the child apologizes.

Repair can sound like:

"I went quiet and made you guess whether I still wanted to be near you. I was upset, and I should have told you I needed space."

"I ignored you after the argument. That was not a fair way to handle anger."

"I am ready to talk now. The limit remains, and the relationship is here."

Name withdrawal because children often experience it as confusing rather than obvious.

When the Child Rejects the Repair

A child may shrug, stay angry, or say, "You always say sorry."

Do not demand forgiveness.

"You do not have to be ready."

"I hear that words are not enough yet."

"I will show the change."

If the complaint is accurate, take it seriously. Repeated apologies without changed behavior can teach the child that repair is a ritual adults use to avoid consequences.

Choose one observable change. Put the phone outside the room during homework. Use a handoff when yelling starts. Stop discussing discipline in the car. Seek professional support. Trust is rebuilt through pattern, not intensity.

When the Same Rupture Happens Again

Repeating a rupture does not automatically make the earlier apology dishonest. It does show that insight alone has not changed the pattern. The next repair should name the repetition directly: "I said I would stop shouting in the car, and it happened again. My plan was not strong enough."

Change the conditions around the behavior rather than making a larger promise. End the conversation before driving, arrange a handoff, remove the recurring trigger where possible, or seek support. If the pattern includes fear, threats, physical force, or prolonged withdrawal, treat it as a safety and support problem, not only a communication problem.

Repair Does Not Require Agreement About Everything

Two people can remember an event differently.

You can say, "I do not remember saying those exact words, and I believe that my tone felt threatening."

You can own the part you know.

"I was louder than I should have been."

Do not use uncertainty to dismiss impact. Also do not confess to an event you genuinely believe did not occur. Repair can hold incomplete information.

Age-Appropriate Repair

With young children, keep it simple.

"I yelled. That was scary. I am sorry. Next time I will use a lower voice."

With school-age children, add impact and plan.

"I embarrassed you in front of your friend. I should have spoken privately. I will do that next time."

With teenagers, respect complexity.

"I read the message without telling you. I was worried, but I violated the privacy agreement. We need a new safety plan, and I need to earn back trust."

Do not disclose graphic details of your own history to explain the rupture. A child can know, "Loud conflict is hard for me because of how I grew up." The child should not be asked to manage the parent's trauma.

Repair With Action

Words matter. Action completes them.

Replace the broken item.

Correct the false statement you made about the child to another person.

Change the family rule if it was unfair.

Ask a co-parent not to defend your behavior.

Schedule help when the same rupture repeats.

A child learns accountability by watching what adults do after they are wrong.

Draft the Repair

Write a repair for one recent moment.

What I did was...

It can have affected you by...

It was my responsibility to...

Next time I will...

You may feel...

Read the draft and remove explanations that reduce responsibility. Keep context only if it helps the child understand the plan.

Grace later added one action. Drinks would stay on a side table, and the laptop would no longer be used at the kitchen table. The new setup protected the device without making a nine-year-old responsible for an adult's panic.

Repair That Changes Something

Repair is not a perfect speech. It is responsibility made visible.

Own the adult behavior before returning to the child's behavior.

Do not require forgiveness, reassurance, or immediate closeness.

An apology gains credibility when the next similar moment contains a different action.

Children do not need proof that parents never fail. They need repeated evidence that failure is not the end of truth or connection.

Chapter 11: Avoid the Permissive Swing

Cycle-breaking can overshoot. A parent raised under rigid control can become so determined not to repeat it that every limit begins to feel like a betrayal.

When Lena was growing up, rules arrived without explanation. A wrong tone could end a conversation. Requests were treated as disrespect. By the time she had children, she had made a private promise: her home would never feel like that.

The promise shaped many loving choices. She listened. She apologized. She tried to understand what sat underneath behavior. It also made it hard to say no.

Her seven-year-old negotiated every bedtime. Her twelve-year-old could cancel family plans by becoming upset. When Lena finally reached her limit, she went from patient to furious and then blamed herself for having limits at all.

The opposite of emotional neglect is not a home without frustration. Children need emotional responsiveness and dependable leadership. Cycle-breaking becomes steadier when warmth and structure work together.

Why Overcorrection Makes Sense

A parent who was controlled, shamed, or emotionally dismissed may confuse authority with domination. A child's disappointment can feel like proof that the parent has become harsh.

That fear can produce several patterns:

> *You explain a limit until the child agrees.*

You reverse a decision when the child becomes distressed.

You avoid age-appropriate responsibilities because you do not want the child to feel pressured.

You allow hurtful behavior because the feeling underneath it is real.

You wait so long to set a boundary that it comes out as anger.

These patterns do not mean you are careless. They often mean your old alarm system treats a child's unhappiness as danger.

Disappointment Is Not Disconnection

A child can be disappointed and still be emotionally seen.

"Your friend cannot sleep over tonight. I know you were hoping she could."

The no remains. The feeling receives company.

This distinction matters because children cannot learn to tolerate ordinary frustration if adults repeatedly remove it. They also cannot learn that feelings are safe if adults punish the feelings. Connected leadership does both jobs: it protects the boundary and stays available for the reaction.

The Warmth-and-Structure Check

When you are unsure whether you are being too rigid or too permissive, ask two questions:

> *Is my child receiving respect, information, and emotional contact?*

Is the adult still carrying the responsibility for safety, schedule, and family limits?

A response can be warm but weak: "I know you are tired, so I guess you do not have to brush your teeth."

A response can be firm but cold: "Stop whining. You are brushing your teeth because I said so."

Connected leadership sounds different: "You are tired and you do not feel like doing it. Teeth still need brushing. Do you want to stand on the stool or sit on the counter?"

The child receives choice inside a limit, not control over whether the limit exists.

Do Not Require Agreement

Parents with a history of emotional neglect can become unusually invested in being understood by their children. They did not receive fair explanations, so they work hard to explain everything.

Explanation is useful. Repeated persuasion is not always useful.

You can say:

> *"I have answered. You do not have to like the answer."*

"I hear that you think this is unfair. The decision is still no."

"I am willing to talk about your feelings. I am not reopening the rule tonight."

This is not dismissive when the child has been heard and the limit is reasonable. It prevents the conversation from becoming a referendum on whether the adult may lead.

Responsibilities Can Be Caring

Expecting a child to contribute is not the same as using the child to meet an adult's emotional needs.

Age-appropriate responsibilities teach membership. A preschooler can carry napkins. A school-age child can put laundry in a basket. A teenager can participate in household tasks and manage increasing parts of their schedule.

The important questions are proportion and role.

Is the task appropriate for the child's age and capacity?

Is the child allowed to have feelings about it?

Does the adult remain responsible for adult problems?

Is love or emotional safety made conditional on performance?

A child who empties the dishwasher is contributing. A child who must manage a parent's mood, mediate adult conflict, or surrender ordinary development to keep the family functioning is carrying an adult role.

Use the Two-Story Pause Before You Give In

When a child protests a limit, your present story may be simple: a screen must turn off, a sibling needs a turn, bedtime has arrived.

The old story may say: If my child is unhappy with me, I am doing harm.

Pause.

What is happening now? My child is disappointed.

What old rule is awake? A loving parent never causes distress.

What does my child need? A calm adult who can tolerate the feeling.

What is the smallest steady action? Keep the limit and reduce my words.

This is one of the places where healing yourself and parenting your child become the same practical task. You learn that another person's displeasure does not automatically mean you have abandoned or harmed them.

When You Have Been Too Permissive

Do not correct the pattern with a dramatic crackdown. Sudden strictness often creates confusion and invites another swing.

Choose one recurring problem. State the new limit clearly. Explain briefly why it is changing. Expect protest.

"We have been letting bedtime move later and later. That is not working for our mornings. Starting tonight, lights are out at nine. I know this is a change, and I will help us get used to it."

Consistency matters more than intensity. A modest limit kept calmly is more useful than a severe limit kept for three days.

Choose One Firm and Kind Limit

Choose one area where guilt has been making the decision for you.

Write:

> *The limit:*
>
> *The reason:*
>
> *The likely feeling:*
>
> *The sentence that acknowledges the feeling:*
>
> *The sentence that keeps the limit:*
>
> *What you will do if the child continues to protest:*
>
> *Example:*
>
> *The limit: No gaming after eight on school nights.*

The reason: Sleep and morning functioning.

The likely feeling: Anger and unfairness.

Acknowledgment: “You wish you had more time.”

Boundary: “The console stays off after eight.”

Follow-through: Keep the device in the common area and stop debating.

Warmth With Structure

Breaking a harsh pattern does not require abandoning authority. Children need adults who can understand feelings without handing every decision to the strongest feeling in the room.

Warmth without structure can leave a child carrying choices that belong to an adult. Structure without warmth can make ordinary dependency feel costly. Connected leadership brings the two together.

Your child is allowed to dislike a limit. You are allowed to remain caring while the dislike is present. The measure is not whether every boundary produces agreement. The measure is whether the boundary is reasonable, clearly held, and free from humiliation or withdrawal.

The work is not to prevent all frustration. It is to show that frustration can happen inside a relationship that remains dependable.

Chapter 12: Parent with Another Adult

Two adults can care about the same child and still disagree about feelings, discipline, privacy, routines, or repair. Cycle-breaking becomes harder when one adult tries to create change while another dismisses the problem or follows a different set of rules.

Andre and his former partner had different rules in different homes. In Andre's house, feelings were discussed. At the other home, the children were expected to "move on" quickly.

Andre worried that every difference would undo his effort. He questioned the children after transitions, corrected their other parent through them, and tried to make his home emotionally perfect.

His eleven-year-old finally said, "Can I just come home without telling you what happened there?"

The request was useful. Andre could not make the other home match his, and his children did not become more willing to report on it. He could offer a responsive home without asking them to become reporters, judges, or proof that his approach was right.

Cycle-breaking often happens in a family system rather than in a private conversation. The goal is not total agreement between adults. It is enough clarity and cooperation to protect the child from adult roles.

Define the Shared Minimum

Adults can differ in style and still agree on a minimum standard.

A useful shared minimum might include:

> *No insults, threats, or physical intimidation.*

No asking a child to carry messages between adults.

No arguing about adult matters through the child.

Clear plans for health, school, safety, and transitions.

Permission for the child to care about every important adult without being tested for loyalty.

Agreement is easier when the request concerns behavior rather than a label.

"You are emotionally unavailable" is likely to produce defense.

"When Maya is upset, can we both avoid telling her she is being ridiculous?" is specific.

Talk About the Pattern Outside the Moment

Do not try to negotiate a parenting philosophy while a child is screaming in the hallway.

Choose a neutral time. Describe what you have observed. Name the shared purpose. Make one request.

"When bedtime stretches past ten, both children are exhausted the next morning. I want evenings to feel calmer for everyone. Can we try starting the routine at eight for the next two weeks?"

Stay with observable events. Avoid turning one conflict into a complete history of the relationship.

Use the Child-Neutral Rule

Before speaking about another caregiver, ask: Does this sentence require the child to defend, condemn, reassure, or choose?

Avoid:

> *"Your dad never listens."*

"Your grandmother is trying to control us."

"Tell your mother that I said no."

Use:

> *"The adults are working out the schedule."*

"You can have different rules there. Here is the rule in this home."

"You do not need to solve this. I will contact the adult."

A child can be told the truth in age-appropriate language without being recruited.

When Another Adult Dismisses Feelings

You may not be able to control what happens in another household. You can still give the child a reliable experience with you.

Do not interrogate the child for evidence. Make room for voluntary disclosure.

"You seem quieter since you got back. I am available if you want to talk."

If the child says, "They told me I was too sensitive," resist the urge to build a case against the other adult.

Try:

> *"That sounds like it hurt."*

"Your feelings make sense to me, even when people understand them differently."

"What would help right now?"

This keeps the focus on the child's experience rather than the adult conflict.

What You Cannot Make Another Adult Do

You cannot force another adult to understand your history, use your preferred language, or repair in the way you would. Repeated attempts to win agreement can pull the child deeper into the conflict.

Focus on conduct you can request or boundaries you can hold: how adults communicate, what information is shared, what happens in your home, and what you will do when safety or dignity is at risk. Significant concerns may require records, professional guidance, legal advice, or specialist support rather than another argument through the child.

Co-Parenting When Contact Is Difficult

In high-conflict situations, extensive emotional discussion between adults may create more harm than cooperation. A businesslike approach can be safer.

Keep communication brief, factual, and focused on the child.

Use written channels when they reduce confusion.

Make requests that can be answered.

Document important health, school, and safety information.

Do not use a child as the communication system.

Where there is coercive control, stalking, threats, or violence, ordinary communication advice may not fit. Safety planning and qualified legal or domestic abuse support may be necessary. A parenting book cannot assess that risk for you.

Partners in the Same Home

A current partner may activate your old defenses in a different way. You might become silent when they are sharp with the child, then criticize them later. Or you may correct every difference because disagreement feels unsafe.

Use a private repair meeting.

Describe the event without exaggeration.

Name what you noticed in yourself.

Identify what the child needed.

Agree on the next response.

"When Theo threw the toy, I froze when voices rose. I know we both wanted the throwing to stop. Next time, can one of us move the toy and the other help his sister step away? We can discuss consequences after everyone is safe."

The aim is not identical reactions. It is coordinated protection and fewer adult conflicts in front of the child.

Extended Family and Old Rules

Grandparents and relatives may expect children to hug, stop crying, keep secrets, or tolerate teasing. You can feel twelve years old while setting a boundary with them.

Prepare the sentence before the visit.

"We do not require hugs. A wave is fine."

"She is allowed to say she is full."

"We do not joke about his body."

"If the teasing continues, we will leave."

Do not make the child enforce the family boundary alone. The adult who recognizes the problem carries the adult conversation.

A Family Decision Filter

When adults disagree, sort the issue into one of three groups.

Safety and dignity: requires a clear boundary.

Health, school, and major routines: needs coordination where possible.

Preference and style: may allow more variation.

A different breakfast, bedtime story, or way of playing is usually a style difference. Humiliation, unsafe supervision, or asking a child to manage adult conflict is not.

This filter prevents you from treating every difference as a threat while still protecting what matters.

Build a One-Page Parenting Agreement

Write one sentence for each area:

> *How we handle intense feelings:*
>
> *How we set and enforce limits:*
>
> *How we speak about other adults:*
>
> *How we communicate schedule or health information:*

> *What we will not ask the child to carry:*
>
> *What we do after an adult loses control:*
>
> *Where we need outside help:*
>
> *The agreement does not need elegant language. It needs observable behavior.*

Parenting Across Adults

You cannot create a completely uniform emotional world for a child. You can create a reliable relationship and protect the child from being used as a messenger, mediator, or loyalty test.

Ask other adults for specific behavior rather than complete agreement with your history or philosophy. Keep adult conflict with adults. Let differences in harmless style remain differences.

When cooperation is limited, return to what is within your control: the tone of your home, the clarity of your boundaries, the truthfulness of your repair, and the support you seek when safety or legal questions exceed a general parenting guide.

Chapter 13: Adapt Across Development

The same emotional principle must change shape as a child develops. Presence that helps a toddler can feel intrusive to a teenager, while distance that respects a teenager can frighten a preschooler.

At three, Noah fell to the floor because the blue cup was in the dishwasher. At nine, he shut his bedroom door after being left out at recess. At fifteen, he answered "fine" and stared at his phone.

His mother, Priya, wanted to respond well at every age. She sometimes mistook the changing surface for a changing need. With the toddler she explained too much. With the school-age child she rushed to fix the friendship. With the teenager she demanded disclosure.

Children's capacities change with development, temperament, language, and context. Emotional responsiveness must change shape too. The task is not to use one perfect script. It is to offer the level of help the child can use now.

Capacity Can Be Uneven

Age does not guarantee the same capacity across language, attention, sensory processing, planning, and stress. A child can manage a task in one setting and need much more support in another. Start with the child's actual functioning rather than a comparison with peers or siblings.

A difference in capacity does not remove every limit. It changes how the limit is taught, cued, and supported. Visual reminders, fewer steps, extra processing time, predictable transitions, or individualized professional guidance can make expectations more usable without lowering the child's dignity.

The Developmental Translation

The same parenting principles look different across ages.

Notice the child's state.

Name only what the child can use.

Provide enough structure for the child's capacity.

Allow increasing agency as skills grow.

Repair in language the child understands.

Developmental expectations are ranges, not deadlines. Children differ, and disability, neurodevelopment, stress, language, culture, and prior experiences can affect what a child can do in a given moment.

Babies and Toddlers: Regulate Through Presence

Very young children rely heavily on adults for rhythm, protection, and help returning from distress. Long explanations are rarely useful during a meltdown.

Use fewer words.

"You wanted the cup."

"You are mad."

"I will not let you hit."

"I am here."

Meet basic needs first. Consider hunger, fatigue, pain, sensory overload, and transition difficulty. Hold the boundary physically and gently when safety requires it.

A responsive answer does not require stopping every cry. Sometimes the adult's job is to remain steady while the child completes the protest.

Preschool Years: Name and Contain

Preschoolers are learning language for feelings, but their impulse control and perspective-taking are still developing. They may know a rule and be unable to use it while highly upset.

Use short sequences:

> *Name: "You are angry that playtime ended."*

Limit: "Blocks are not for throwing."

Alternative: "You can stomp here or help me put them in the box."

Do not ask a flooded four-year-old, "Why did you do that?" The child may not know. Ask later, when curiosity is possible.

Offer limited choices that both work for the adult:

> *"Walk to the car or hold my hand."*

"Red pajamas or green."

Too many choices can create more load rather than more agency.

School-Age Children: Add Meaning and Skill

School-age children can often reflect after the event, compare perspectives, and practice a plan. They may also become intensely concerned with fairness and belonging.

Begin with listening before advice.

"Do you want me to listen, help you think, or help you act?"

Break a problem into what is controllable and what is not.

Practice language for peers, teachers, and siblings.

Help the child notice body signals and early warning signs.

Keep family responsibilities clear and age-appropriate.

A child who says "Nobody likes me" may not need immediate contradiction. "Today felt lonely" creates contact. Later you can look at the evidence together without arguing with the feeling.

Early Adolescence: Respect the Door Without Disappearing

A young adolescent can want privacy and support at the same time. Repeated questioning can feel intrusive, especially when the child is still forming the experience.

Try an open door with a time anchor.

"You do not have to talk now. I will check in after dinner."

"I can listen without contacting anyone, unless I am worried about safety."

"Would it be easier to walk, text, or talk in the car?"

Privacy is not the same as secrecy about danger. A parent still has responsibility for safety, health, and appropriate supervision.

Later Adolescence: Move From Manager to Consultant

Older adolescents need increasing practice making decisions, living with proportionate consequences, and asking for help.

A consultant does not disappear. A consultant asks before taking over.

"What have you tried?"

"What part do you want help with?"

"Do you want my opinion, or do you want me to listen first?"

"What is your plan if that does not work?"

Keep a small number of clear household and safety limits. Avoid controlling every preference. The aim is not obedience at eighteen. It is growing judgment, responsibility, and a relationship in which help can still be requested.

When Your Child's Age Activates Your Own History

A child's developmental stage may match an age at which something painful happened to you. The reaction can arrive as irritation, fear, grief, or urgency.

A five-year-old's dependence may awaken memories of being told to manage alone.

A twelve-year-old's independence can feel like rejection.

A teenager's disagreement may activate old punishment or abandonment fears.

Use the Two-Story Pause.

What is the developmental task in front of me?

What did this age mean in my family?

What am I tempted to require from my child because of that history?

What would support the child I actually have?

You do not need a complete memory to notice the pattern.

Siblings Need Fairness, Not Sameness

Children of different ages and capacities will not receive identical rules.

A seven-year-old may need an adult beside them to start homework. A fourteen-year-old may manage the schedule but need help breaking down a major project.

Explain difference without comparing worth.

"Your brother has a different bedtime because he is older."

"She gets help with transitions because that is hard for her. You receive help in other areas."

Do not turn one child into the mature helper by default. Competence is not consent to carry the family.

Developmental Repair

Repair also changes with age.

For a toddler: "I was too loud. That scared you. I am sorry." Then reconnect through calm presence.

For a school-age child: name the action, impact, and next step. Invite a brief response.

For an adolescent: respect complexity and allow time. "I interrupted and mocked your idea. That was disrespectful. I am sorry. You can tell me more now or later."

Do not demand immediate forgiveness at any age.

Translate One Principle

Choose a principle such as validation, limit-setting, or repair.

Write how it would sound for:

> *A toddler:*
>
> *A six-year-old:*
>
> *A ten-year-old:*
>
> *A fourteen-year-old:*

Then remove half the words from the youngest version. For the oldest version, add choice and privacy without giving up safety.

Development Changes the Response

The child in front of you keeps changing. Emotional responsiveness must grow with them.

Young children need more borrowed calm and simple structure. School-age children can add reflection and skill. Adolescents need increasing privacy, agency, and consultation, while adults keep responsibility for safety.

Use age as a guide, not a verdict. Temperament, disability, stress, language, and context matter. When a developmental stage activates your own past, separate what this age meant for you from what this child needs now.

The principle stays stable: see the child, hold the adult role, and adjust the form of help to the capacity available in this moment.

Chapter 14: Build a Responsive Home

A responsive home is built less by one perfect conversation than by the responses family members learn to expect on ordinary days.

The most important conversation in Marisol's family did not happen at a family meeting. It happened on a Tuesday when everyone was late.

Her son could not find his shoes. Her daughter had remembered a form that needed a signature. Marisol felt the familiar pressure rise. In her childhood, lateness led to blame and silence.

She almost shouted, "Why does everything depend on me?"

Instead she said, "We are having a hard morning. Shoes first. We will solve the form in the car."

No one applauded. They were still late. But the family did not have to recover from an attack as well as a rushed morning.

A responsive family culture is built from repeated ordinary moments. It does not require constant emotional discussion. It requires patterns that make feelings speakable, limits predictable, repair normal, and adult responsibility visible.

Culture Lives in Repetition

Children learn what a family believes by what happens repeatedly.

What happens when someone cries?

What happens when someone says no?

What happens when an adult is wrong?

What happens when plans fail?

What happens when two people want different things?

A family can have wonderful values written on the wall and still teach that feelings are dangerous if adults withdraw whenever discomfort appears.

Family culture shifts when a different response is repeated often enough that people begin to expect it.

Create Predictable Points of Contact

Connection does not need to be elaborate.

A greeting at reunion.

Ten minutes beside a child before bed.

A weekly walk.

A question at dinner that does not require a performance.

A short check-in after a difficult transition.

Predictable contact matters because it is not dependent on the child earning attention through crisis or achievement.

Choose rituals that fit the family's actual life. A complicated routine that produces resentment is less useful than a simple one that survives busy weeks.

Make Feelings Speakable, Not Mandatory

An emotionally responsive home does not require everyone to discuss every feeling.

Offer invitations.

"What was one easy part and one hard part of today?"

"Do you want company or space?"

"Is there something you want us to understand before we plan?"

Accept "I do not know" or "not now" when safety is not at issue.

Forced disclosure can turn emotional openness into another demand. The child learns more from an available adult who respects timing than from a compulsory nightly interrogation.

Use Family Language Consistently

A few shared phrases can lower conflict because they shorten the path back to the principle.

"Feelings are allowed. Harm is not."

"The limit is staying. I am staying too."

"Listen, help, or act?"

"Pause before the second sentence."

"We can repair this."

These phrases should not become slogans used to avoid real listening. They work when adult behavior supports them.

Hold Family Meetings That Solve One Thing

A useful family meeting is brief and concrete.

Name one problem.

Invite each person to describe what is happening.

Identify what belongs with adults.

Choose one experiment.

Decide when to review it.

Example:

> *Problem: Mornings become loud and rushed.*

Children notice: They cannot find belongings and feel blamed.

Adults own: The schedule starts too late, and instructions come all at once.

Experiment: Pack bags at night, place shoes by the door, use a three-item morning list.

Review: Sunday afternoon.

Do not turn the meeting into a trial. The goal is not to identify the most difficult family member. It is to change a repeatable pattern.

Protect One-to-One Relationships

Family culture includes the individual bond between each child and caregiver.

A child may need a small pocket of attention that is not shared with siblings. This does not have to be equal by the minute. It should be sufficiently reliable that no child must create a crisis to receive individual contact.

For a busy parent, one-to-one time might be a grocery trip, a bedtime rotation, a short drive, or a monthly breakfast. Name it so the child can anticipate it.

Let the Home Contain Adult Feelings Without Assigning Them

Children can know that adults have feelings. They should not become responsible for managing them.

Appropriate: "I am disappointed about work. I am going to take a walk and call a friend."

Burdening: "You need to behave because I cannot take one more problem."

Appropriate: "I am sad today, and it is not your job to fix it."

Burdening: silent withdrawal that makes the child guess what they did.

The aim is not emotional invisibility. It is ownership. The adult names enough truth to reduce confusion and directs adult needs toward adult support.

Plan for Stress Before Stress Arrives

Every family has predictable pressure points: school mornings, holidays, travel, illness, custody transitions, bedtime, homework, public outings.

Use a before plan.

What usually activates the parent?

What usually overloads the child?

Which expectations can be simplified?

What words will the adult use?

Where is the exit or pause?

Who can help?

A plan does not guarantee calm. It reduces the number of decisions made while everyone is already overloaded.

Celebrate Repair, Not Performance

Families often celebrate achievement and good behavior. A cycle-breaking home can also notice relationship skills.

"You came back and told the truth."

"You were angry and kept your hands safe."

"We disagreed and found a plan."

"I was wrong, and we repaired it."

Avoid turning these observations into praise that pressures the child to be emotionally mature for the adults. Notice the skill without assigning a fixed identity.

Review the Family Culture Without Shame

Once a month, ask:

> *What helped us feel connected?*

Where did we keep getting stuck?

Which limit became unclear?

Who needs more support?

What should adults change first?

Do not ask whether the family is healthy or unhealthy as a single verdict. Look for one pattern to keep and one pattern to adjust.

Make a Responsive Home Plan

Complete these lines:

> *Our two most difficult daily moments are:*
>
> *Our simplest point of daily connection will be:*

> *The family phrase we will practice is:*
>
> *One limit that needs clearer follow-through is:*
>
> *One adult need that should move to adult support is:*
>
> *The repair practice we want children to see is:*
>
> *We will review this plan on:*
>
> *Put the plan somewhere private and usable, not somewhere it becomes a display of family problems.*

Building the Home Culture

A responsive home is not a home in which everyone is calm, expressive, and available at all times. It is a home with recognizable ways to return.

Children benefit from predictable contact, speakable feelings, dependable limits, and adults who own adult needs. Small family phrases, brief meetings, and preparation for known pressure points can turn values into behavior.

The culture changes through repetition. One Tuesday morning does not define a family. A pattern of blame can be interrupted. A pattern of repair can become familiar. The work is ordinary, and that is why it can last.

Chapter 15: Know When Help Is Needed

Knowing when to seek help is not a test of how severe a problem looks from the outside. More useful questions are how long it has lasted, how much it disrupts daily life, whether it is worsening, and whether anyone is unsafe.

After months of difficult mornings, Jamal began planning every family activity around preventing his daughter's distress. She had stopped attending school regularly, slept poorly, and panicked when he left the room.

Jamal kept telling himself that he should be able to handle it. He had read parenting books. He was trying to stay calm. Asking for help felt like admitting that he had repeated his own parents' failures.

The more useful question was not whether he was a good enough parent. It was whether the family needed more support than one parent could provide alone.

A book can offer education, language, and practice. It cannot assess a child, treat a mental health condition, evaluate immediate danger, or replace individualized care. Seeking appropriate support is not a failure of cycle-breaking. It is one of the ways adults carry adult responsibility.

Look at Duration, Intensity, and Impairment

Children have strong feelings. A difficult week is not automatically a disorder.

Consider professional input when a pattern is persistent, intense, worsening, or interfering with daily life. Areas of impairment may include:

> *School attendance or learning.*

Sleep, eating, or physical functioning.

Friendships and ordinary activities.

Family safety.

The child's ability to recover after distress.

The caregiver's ability to provide safe, consistent care.

The Centers for Disease Control and Prevention notes that persistent or extreme fears, or worries that interfere with home, school, or play, warrant a conversation with a healthcare provider about evaluation. An assessment can help clarify what is happening and what support fits (Centers for Disease Control and Prevention, 2026).

Seek Urgent Help for Safety Concerns

Urgent action may be needed when a child or adult is in immediate danger, has serious injuries, cannot be kept safe, expresses intent to die or seriously harm someone, or shows other signs of an acute crisis.

Contact local emergency services or an appropriate crisis service in your country. Do not rely on a book, online forum, or delayed appointment when immediate safety is at risk.

For suspected abuse or neglect, follow the reporting and protection requirements in your location. Laws and services differ, so obtain current local guidance.

Choose the Right Starting Point

Depending on the concern, a starting point may be:

> *The child's pediatrician or primary-care clinician.*

A licensed child or family mental health professional.

The school counselor, psychologist, or special education team.

A developmental or neurodevelopmental evaluation service.

A domestic abuse service for coercion, threats, or violence.

A local parenting or family support program.

A qualified legal professional for custody or safety orders.

You do not need to know the final diagnosis or service before asking a first question.

Prepare for an Appointment

Bring observations rather than conclusions.

When did the pattern begin?

Where does it happen?

How often and how long?

What seems to come before it?

What helps or worsens it?

How are sleep, eating, school, play, and relationships affected?

What changes or stressors have occurred?

What safety concerns are present?

Include strengths. A clear picture contains what the child can do, where the child functions well, and which relationships or settings help.

Avoid presenting the child as the family problem. Describe the interaction and context.

Ask What the Help Will Involve

A useful professional relationship should provide enough clarity for informed participation.

You can ask:

> *What is your understanding of the concern?*

What assessment is being proposed?

What goals would we work toward?

How will caregivers be involved?

How will progress be reviewed?

What are the likely benefits, limits, and alternatives?

What should we do if risk increases?

For parenting interventions, research reviews suggest that approaches which explicitly address caregiver emotion regulation, stress, and reflective capacity may be useful, though the evidence varies by program and population (Camoirano, 2017; Huynh et al., 2024). No single approach fits every family.

Get Help for the Parent Too

Sometimes the child's behavior is the visible reason for seeking support, while the parent is carrying panic, grief, rage, numbness, or exhaustion that also needs care.

Adult support might include individual therapy, a parenting program, a peer group, medical care, practical respite, or help from trusted people.

Choose support that does not make the child responsible for the parent's recovery. A parent can say, "I am getting help with my strong reactions," without sharing details the child must hold.

When Services Are Hard to Access

Cost, waiting lists, location, language, disability access, insurance, and cultural fit can make support difficult to obtain.

Ask primary-care or school professionals for referral options.

Contact community mental health centers or local family services.

Ask providers about sliding fees, groups, telehealth, or cancellation lists.

Request interpretation or accessible communication when needed.

Document concerns and the help you have sought.

Use emergency or crisis services when risk becomes immediate.

These steps do not solve structural barriers. They can create more entry points.

Evaluate Advice Carefully

Parenting information can sound confident while offering little evidence or no room for individual differences.

Be cautious when advice:

> *Promises guaranteed outcomes.*

Blames one person for every problem.

Encourages secrecy or isolation.

Dismisses medical, developmental, or safety concerns.

Uses fear to sell a single method.

Asks a child to provide emotional care for the parent.

A credible professional should be able to explain scope, training, confidentiality, fees, and the basis for recommendations. Verify licenses and complaint procedures through the appropriate local regulator where relevant.

When Your Own Behavior Frightens You

Take it seriously if you fear you may hurt your child, cannot stop escalating, use physical force, drive dangerously while angry, threaten abandonment, or repeatedly become unavailable for long periods.

Create distance from immediate danger when possible. Ask another safe adult to take over. Remove weapons or other means of harm from the situation. Contact emergency, crisis, medical, or mental health services according to the level of risk.

Shame may urge secrecy. Safety requires disclosure to an appropriate person.

Create a Support Decision Page

Concern:

> *How long it has been happening:*

> *Where it interferes with daily life:*
>
> *Immediate safety risk, if any:*
>
> *What we have tried:*
>
> *What helps:*
>
> *Who could be a first contact:*
>
> *Questions to bring:*
>
> *What support the parent needs:*
>
> *Date for next action:*
>
> *Do not use the page to postpone urgent action. It is for organizing a non-immediate next step.*

Deciding When to Seek Help

Ordinary family difficulty does not always require professional treatment. Persistent, severe, worsening, or impairing concerns deserve assessment. Immediate danger deserves immediate action.

Seeking help is not proof that you have failed. It is a way of matching the level of support to the level of need.

Bring observations, ask clear questions, and include the parent's needs in the plan. A responsive parent does not have to become the child's therapist, diagnostician, or entire support system. The adult task is to notice when the family needs more than the family can currently provide and to help open the next door.

Conclusion: Good Enough, Still Growing

The promise of cycle-breaking can become another form of pressure.

You may begin with a sincere desire to give your child what you did not receive, then discover an impossible private standard: notice every feeling, respond calmly every time, never repeat a harmful phrase, heal your history quickly enough that it never enters the room.

That standard does not create emotional responsiveness. It creates vigilance and shame.

The work in this book rests on a steadier idea. Your child needs to be seen often enough, protected clearly enough, and repaired with honestly enough to know that feelings can exist inside a dependable relationship. You need practices that work on ordinary mornings, during arguments, and after the moment you wish you could redo.

The Two-Story Pause gives you a place to return:

> *What is happening in the room right now?*

What old rule or fear has awakened in me?

What does my child need from the adult in this moment?

What is the smallest steady action I can take next?

Sometimes the steady action is a breath and one fewer sentence. Sometimes it is a clear no. Sometimes it is moving a child or object to keep people safe. Sometimes it is saying, "I was wrong." Sometimes it is calling a professional because the problem exceeds what a book or family can manage alone.

What Changes First

Change can appear in small forms before it appears in calm behavior.

You notice your body tighten before you shout.

You recognize that a child's tears are not a verdict on your parenting.

You stop explaining a limit after the answer is clear.

You return to a child without asking the child to rescue you from shame.

You ask another adult for help before resentment hardens.

These are not minor achievements. They are changes in the sequence that creates family life.

A child does not need to understand your history to benefit from your work. The child benefits when your history has less power to decide the next sentence.

Keep the Child Out of the Healing Role

Your own healing matters. It also belongs with adults, private reflection, and appropriate professional support.

The child does not need to know every reason a moment was hard for you. A simple truth is often enough.

"I got overwhelmed. That was not your fault."

"I am working on staying present when feelings are strong."

"You do not need to take care of me."

This protects the relationship from reversing roles while allowing the child to see responsible growth.

Choose One Practice to Keep

Do not try to maintain every worksheet at once.

Choose the tool that addressed your most common pattern.

The trigger map, if reactions seem to arrive without warning.

The first ninety seconds, if you need a usable pause.

Listen, help, or act, if you solve too quickly.

The connected limit, if guilt makes boundaries collapse.

The five-part repair, if shame makes you avoid returning.

The responsive home plan, if the family needs a few shared routines.

Practice one tool long enough for it to become familiar. Add another when the first can survive a difficult week.

Measure Direction, Not Purity

Ask:

> *Are feelings becoming more speakable?*

Are limits becoming more predictable?

Are adult mistakes being named more honestly?

Is the child carrying less responsibility for adult emotion?

Are we seeking help sooner when safety or functioning declines?

No family answers yes every day. Look for direction across time.

The past may still appear. A voice, posture, or silence may return before you recognize it. That does not erase the work. Notice, stop, repair, and learn what the moment exposed.

Cycle-breaking is not the production of a child who is never hurt, angry, disappointed, or confused. It is the creation of a family in which those experiences do not automatically lead to humiliation, abandonment, or role reversal.

You are not required to become a flawless parent in order to become a more available one. Return to the room you are actually in. See the child who is actually there. Carry the adult responsibility that is yours. Then take the smallest steady action you can sustain.

Appendix A: The Two-Story Pause Workbook

Use this worksheet after a difficult moment or before a predictable one. It is not a test of whether your reaction was reasonable. It is a way to separate information that became tangled under pressure.

Step 1 Record the Present Story

Write only what a camera and microphone could have captured.

What happened?

What did the child say or do?

What did you say or do?

What immediate safety or practical issue was present?

Avoid labels such as manipulative, lazy, dramatic, disrespectful, or selfish. Replace the label with behavior.

Instead of: "She was manipulative."

Write: "She cried, asked five more times, and said I did not love her after I said the visit was over."

Step 2 Record the Old Story

Complete the sentences that fit.

In my childhood, needing help meant:

> *Strong feelings were treated as:*
>
> *A child who said no was:*
>
> *Adults reacted to mistakes by:*
>
> *I learned that a good child should:*
>
> *I learned that a good parent should:*
>
> *The fear underneath my reaction was:*
>
> *The old rule that appeared was:*

> *You are looking for a learned meaning, not a perfect memory.*

Step 3 Identify the Child's Present Need

A need is not the same as a demand.

Possible needs include:

> *Safety.*

Information.

Comfort.

Help organizing a task.

A limit held clearly.

Time to recover.

A chance to try again.

Protection from humiliation.

Space without abandonment.

A developmentally appropriate choice.

What did the child appear to need from the adult role?

What did the child request that you could not or should not provide?

What feeling could be acknowledged without changing the decision?

Step 4 Choose the Smallest Steady Action

Choose one action that is available at your actual level of activation.

Reduce words.

Lower volume.

Move closer or farther away.

Remove an unsafe object.

Name one feeling.

State one limit.

Offer two acceptable choices.

Ask whether the child wants listening, help, or action.

Take a brief pause while another safe adult stays present.

Return and repair.

Request outside help.

Write the exact sentence or action:

Step 5 Review Without Prosecution

What worked even slightly?

Where did the old story take over?

What did the child learn from the adult response?

Is a repair needed?

What would make this moment 10 percent easier next time?

The purpose of review is to improve the sequence. Shame tells you to produce a verdict about your character. Practice asks what can change at the next decision point.

Appendix B: Trigger and Recovery Map

A trigger map helps you prepare for repeat situations without treating the child as the problem.

Part 1 Common Trigger Areas

Mark any situation that often produces shutdown, anger, panic, or urgent fixing.

Crying that continues after comfort.

Clinginess or repeated bids for attention.

A child saying no.

Whining or repeated requests.

Public behavior that attracts attention.

Sibling conflict.

Mess, spills, or broken objects.

Slow transitions.

Bedtime resistance.

School refusal or homework conflict.

A child withdrawing or closing a door.

A teenager challenging a rule.

Another adult criticizing your parenting.

Noise, touch, or sensory overload.

Financial or time pressure.

Part 2 Your Early Signals

Body signals:

> *Jaw or shoulders tighten.*

Face becomes hot.

Chest or throat feels constricted.

Breathing becomes shallow.

Hands shake or clench.

You feel suddenly tired or far away.

Thought signals:

> *"This has to stop now."*

"No one respects me."

"I cannot handle one more thing."

"My child will become impossible."

"I am exactly like my parent."

Behavior signals:

> *Repeating the same instruction.*

Talking faster.

Adding old grievances.

Sarcasm or threats.

Leaving without saying when you will return.

Trying to purchase peace with a reward.

Demanding an apology before the child is ready.

Circle your earliest reliable signal. That is the best place for the pause.

Part 3 Your Recovery Menu

Select three options that are realistic in your home.

Put both feet on the floor.

Exhale longer than you inhale once or twice.

Use cold water on your hands.

Say, "I need a minute before I answer."

Look at one neutral object and describe it silently.

Move the conversation to a quieter place.

Ask another adult to take over.

Read a prepared sentence from your phone.

Delay a non-urgent consequence.

Eat, drink water, or address a physical need.

Step outside only when the child remains safely supervised.

Contact an appropriate support person.

Part 4 The Return Plan

A pause is not complete until the adult returns or communicates what happens next.

My return sentence:

> *The maximum time I can reasonably request:*
>
> *Who can remain with the child if needed:*
>
> *What I will do if I am still unable to respond safely:*
>
> *What repair will sound like if I used a harmful tone:*

Part 5 Prevention

The trigger is not always solved in the emotional moment.

What practical change could reduce frequency?

Earlier bedtime.

Fewer transitions.

A visible schedule.

Snacks before errands.

Less rushed departure time.

Noise reduction.

Shared caregiving.

Clearer screen rules.

Adult treatment or support.

A school or developmental evaluation.

Choose one prevention change to test for two weeks. Record whether it changes the pattern rather than assuming success or failure after one day.

Appendix C: Scripts for Difficult Moments

Scripts are starting language, not lines a child must accept. Use fewer words when either person is highly activated.

When a Child Is Crying

"You wanted this to go differently."

"I am here. You do not have to stop crying for me."

"I cannot change the answer. I can stay with you while it is hard."

"Do you want closeness or a little space?"

When a Child Is Clingy

"You want to stay close."

"I am going to the kitchen, and I will come back after I put the dishes away."

"You can hold my hand while we walk in."

"Goodbye is hard today. Your caregiver will help you, and I will return after lunch."

When a Child Is Angry

"You are angry. I will listen when bodies are safe."

"You may say you hate the rule. You may not hit."

"I am moving the toy because it is being thrown."

"Do you want space, water, or help getting the words out?"

When the Answer Is No

"I know you wanted yes. The answer is no."

"You do not have to agree. The limit is staying."

"I have answered. I can talk about the disappointment, not reopen the decision."

"You can choose between these two options."

When a Child Says You Are Mean

"It feels mean to you because I stopped something you wanted."

"You are allowed to be angry with me."

"I will think about whether the limit was fair. I am not changing it while we are shouting."

When You Need a Pause

"I am getting too sharp. I am taking one minute, and I will come back."

"I want to answer without yelling. I need a pause."

"I am not leaving the problem. I am making enough room to handle it safely."

When You Have Shouted

"I shouted. That was frightening and not okay."

"You did not cause my yelling. Your behavior still needs a limit, and my yelling was my responsibility."

"I am sorry. Next time I will stop talking and take a pause before I answer."

"You do not have to forgive me immediately."

When You Froze or Withdrew

"I went quiet and left you guessing. I was overwhelmed, but I should have told you I needed a break."

"I am ready to listen now."

"I can see that my silence felt like I was gone from the relationship."

When a Child Does Not Want to Talk

"You do not have to talk now."

"I will check again after dinner."

"You can write or text me if that is easier."

"I will respect privacy unless I am concerned about safety."

When Advice Is Not Wanted

"Do you want me to listen, help you think, or help take action?"

"I have an idea. Would you like to hear it?"

"I can stay with you without solving it."

When Adults Disagree

"The adults will handle the disagreement."

"You do not need to take sides."

"Rules may differ between homes. I will explain the rule here."

"I will contact the other adult. You do not need to carry the message."

When Extended Family Crosses a Boundary

"We do not require hugs."

"Please do not joke about her body."

"He is allowed to leave the table when he is finished."

"If the teasing continues, we will end the visit."

When You Need Professional Support

"This has been hard for long enough that we are going to get more help."

"You are not in trouble. We want to understand what would make daily life easier and safer."

"I am also getting help with my reactions. That is an adult responsibility."

A Script Check

Before using a script, ask:

> *Is it true?*

Is it brief enough for this state?

Does it keep adult responsibility with the adult?

Does it acknowledge the feeling without promising the requested outcome?

Does it avoid asking the child to comfort me?

A plain sentence delivered consistently is more useful than a perfect sentence delivered as a performance.

Appendix D: Repair Worksheet

Use this after shouting, insulting, withdrawing, using excessive force, making an unfair accusation, or failing to protect a child's dignity. For serious or repeated harm, repair must include changed behavior and appropriate professional or safety support.

1 Describe the Adult Action

Write the action without euphemism.

"I yelled."

"I called her selfish."

"I grabbed his wrist harder than necessary."

"I ignored him for the rest of the evening."

"I told her she was just like her other parent."

2 Describe the Likely Impact

Use modest, accurate language.

"It can have scared you."

"It put you in the middle of an adult conflict."

"It made it seem as though your feelings were the problem."

"It left you unsure whether I would speak to you again."

Do not claim to know exactly what the child felt. Invite correction.

3 Remove the Defense

Explanations belong after responsibility, and some do not belong in the repair.

Cross out:

> *"But you kept pushing."*

"But I had a terrible day."

"But you know better."

"But my parent did worse."

Write:

> *"My stress explains why I was vulnerable to losing control. It does not make the behavior your responsibility."*

4 State the Change

A repair is stronger when the next action is concrete.

"I will move away from the argument before I shout."

"I will not use your other parent as an insult."

"I will ask another adult to take over when I feel unsafe."

"I am contacting a counselor because this has happened more than once."

5 Make Room for the Child

Possible invitations:

> *"Is there anything you want me to understand?"*

"You can tell me now or later."

"You do not have to make me feel better."

"What would help restore safety?"

The child may be quiet, angry, skeptical, or uninterested. The adult can still complete the repair.

6 Address the Original Behavior Separately

Write the child's behavior or family problem that still needs attention.

Then write the later boundary.

"I am sorry I screamed. The rule about coming home on time still needs to be addressed. We will discuss it after dinner."

This prevents apology from erasing leadership and discipline from erasing responsibility.

7 Track Repetition

Has this behavior happened before?

What happens immediately before it?

What prevention step has been tried?

What support is needed now?

A repeated apology without a meaningful change can become part of the harmful pattern. Use repetition as information that more support or a stronger safety plan is needed.

Appendix E: A Thirty-Day Cycle-Breaking Practice

This plan is deliberately small. Repeat days when needed. Skip any exercise that is unsafe or unsuitable for your family.

Week 1 Notice

Day 1: Write the three child behaviors that activate you most.

Day 2: Identify your earliest body signal.

Day 3: Record one old family rule about needs.

Day 4: Replace one label with a camera description.

Day 5: Notice one moment when your child sought connection indirectly.

Day 6: Use the Two-Story Pause after, not during, a difficult moment.

Day 7: Review what you noticed without choosing a new rule yet.

Week 2 Pause

Day 8: Practice one longer exhale when nothing difficult is happening.

Day 9: Put a pause sentence in your phone.

Day 10: Reduce one instruction from three sentences to one.

Day 11: Move an adult need toward adult support.

Day 12: Ask another caregiver for one specific form of help.

Day 13: Use a brief pause and state when you will return.

Day 14: Review which pause was usable, not which looked calmest.

Week 3 Connect and Lead

Day 15: Reflect one feeling before giving advice.

Day 16: Ask, "Listen, help, or act?"

Day 17: Hold one small limit without adding a lecture.

Day 18: Offer two acceptable choices inside a boundary.

Day 19: Allow a child's disappointment without changing the answer.

Day 20: Create ten minutes of predictable one-to-one contact.

Day 21: Review whether warmth and structure were both present.

Week 4 Repair and Build Culture

Day 22: Repair one small rupture without using "but."

Day 23: Tell a child one adult feeling without assigning it to them.

Day 24: Choose one family phrase.

Day 25: Prepare a plan for a predictable pressure point.

Day 26: Hold a brief family meeting about one practical problem.

Day 27: Notice a child's relationship skill without assigning a fixed identity.

Day 28: Complete the Responsive Home Plan.

Day 29: Identify whether any concern needs professional assessment.

Day 30: Choose the one practice you will continue for the next month.

Monthly Review

What became easier to notice?

Which old rule appeared most often?

Which child behavior still creates the most difficulty?

Which limit needs more clarity?

Which repair needs a changed behavior behind it?

What support does the parent need?

What is the smallest steady action for the next month?

The purpose of thirty days is not to complete your healing. It is to establish a repeatable way to notice, pause, connect, lead, and return.

References

Camoirano, A. (2017). Mentalizing makes parenting work: A review about parental reflective functioning and clinical interventions to improve it. Frontiers in Psychology, 8, Article 14. https://doi.org/10.3389/fpsyg.2017.00014

Center on the Developing Child at Harvard University. (n.d.). Serve and return. Retrieved August 5, 2026, from https://developingchild.harvard.edu/key-concept/serve-and-return/

Centers for Disease Control and Prevention. (2026, May 15). Anxiety and depression in children. https://www.cdc.gov/children-mental-health/about/about-anxiety-and-depression-in-children.html

Edler, K., & Valentino, K. (2024). Parental self-regulation and engagement in emotion socialization: A systematic review. Psychological Bulletin, 150(2), 154-191. https://doi.org/10.1037/bul0000423

England-Mason, G., Andrews, K., Atkinson, L., & Gonzalez, A. (2023). Emotion socialization parenting interventions targeting emotional competence in young children: A systematic review and meta-analysis of randomized controlled trials. Clinical Psychology Review, 100, Article 102252. https://doi.org/10.1016/j.cpr.2023.102252

Greene, C. A., Haisley, L., Wallace, C., & Ford, J. D. (2020). Intergenerational effects of childhood maltreatment: A systematic review of the parenting practices of adult survivors of childhood abuse, neglect, and violence. Clinical Psychology Review, 80, Article 101891. https://doi.org/10.1016/j.cpr.2020.101891

Havighurst, S. S., Radovini, A., Hao, B., & Kehoe, C. E. (2020). Emotion-focused parenting interventions for prevention and treatment of child and adolescent mental health problems: A review of recent literature. Current Opinion in Psychiatry, 33(6), 586-601. https://doi.org/10.1097/YCO.0000000000000647

Huynh, T., Kerr, M. L., Kim, C. N., Fourianalistyawati, E., Chang, V. Y.-R., & Duncan, L. G. (2024). Parental reflective capacities: A scoping review of mindful parenting and parental reflective functioning. Mindfulness, 15, 1531-1602. https://doi.org/10.1007/s12671-024-02379-6

Pianka, G. A. (2025). Validate, validate, validate. In Coaching families for resilience: How pediatricians can support caregivers and prevent burnout. American Academy of Pediatrics. https://doi.org/10.1542/9781610027892-appv

Tronick, E., & Beeghly, M. (2011). Infants' meaning-making and the development of mental health problems. American Psychologist, 66(2), 107-119. https://doi.org/10.1037/a0021631

About the Author

Clara Rowan Fielding writes practical, research-informed guides for adults who want to change difficult family patterns without turning everyday life into a therapy session. Her work favors clear language, realistic examples, steady boundaries, and tools that can be used in the middle of an ordinary week.

In this book, she brings those priorities to the dual task of raising emotionally seen children while taking responsibility for the old defenses that parenting can expose.

www.ingramcontent.com/pod-product-compliance
Lightning Source LLC
LaVergne TN
LVHW021737071126
851857LV00040B/1479